# THE PRESIDENCY IN FLUX

GEORGE E. REEDY

# THE
# PRESIDENCY
# IN FLUX

COLUMBIA UNIVERSITY PRESS
NEW YORK & LONDON 1973

Library of Congress Cataloging in Publication Data

Reedy, George E     1917–
    The Presidency in flux

    (Pegram lecture series, 1972)
    1.   Presidents—United States—Addresses, essays,
lectures.   I. Title.   II. Series.
JK515.R4        329′.00973      73-2580
ISBN 0-231-03736-8

*The George B. Pegram Lectures*

During and since the World War II, science has come to occupy an unprecedented position within our political institutions. In the conduct of war and international relations, in the exploration of space, in the exploitation of the commons of the high seas, science has brought to the Presidency instruments and potentialities of awesome power and variety.

It is no longer possible to speak of separate categories such as science and society, or of a government of men free of scientific or technological considerations. Our new knowledge, our expanded means, demand new institutions, or responsible changes in our old ones.

Such an institution as the Presidency reveals the critical nature of this modern problem. The same responsibilities remain, and yet the modes of decision making have changed but little, and the forces, such as science, which are remaking the world, are yet to be fully understood at the center of our democracy.

Mr. George E. Reedy, who was intimately involved in the Office of the President during Lyndon Johnson's term of office, presents his view of the problem in this George B. Pegram series.

The lectureship was named to honor George Braxton Pegram (1877–1958), one of the most influential scientists of the nuclear age. He was Professor of Physics, Dean, and Vice President of Columbia University. He was instrumental in seeing that the government was aware of the potentialities of nuclear energy in the defense of the country. In 1946 he headed the Initiatory University Group which proposed that a regional center for research in the nuclear sciences be established in the New York area and thus played a key role in the establishment of Associated Universities, Inc., and the founding of Brookhaven National Laboratory. He received many awards and honorary degrees, the last of which was the Karl Taylor Compton gold medal for distinguished service in physics. George B. Pegram's lucid mind and gentle ways will be long remembered by those who knew him. This series has been established to further his conviction that the results of science can be made to serve the needs and hopes of mankind.

George E. Reedy was born in East Chicago in 1917 and received a B.A. in Sociology from the University of Chicago in 1938. From 1938 to 1951 he served as correspondent for United Press in Washington, interrupted only by war service in the Pacific 1942–1946. During those years he covered both houses of Congress. From 1951 to 1968 he worked in the government as consultant and appointed official in Senate committees, and later in the White House.

He is known as the author of *Who Will Do Our Fighting for Us* (1969), and *The Twilight of the Presidency* (1970). While his credentials point to a man of action, his books reveal a scholar and a shrewd observer of human affairs.

Mr. Reedy delivered the lectures on which this volume is based in November 1971 while a Fellow of the Woodrow Wilson International Center for Scholars. He has since accepted an appointment as Dean of the College of Journalism of Marquette University.

THE 1971 PEGRAM LECTURESHIP COMMITTEE
Garman Harbottle
Geoffrey Hind
William Marcuse
Virginia Sayre
Maxwell Small
Knud Knudsen (Chairman)

# CONTENTS

# CHAPTER 1

## THE AGE OF
## MASS SOCIETY

I WISH TO OPERATE here on the premise that a man who is speaking to posterity does not really need to wait for the audience. Therefore, it is my intention to set forth some basic theses and then open the floor for discussion, for I have never yet been convinced that the people to whom I am talking really understand what I am saying until they have had an opportunity to ask me some questions.

My basic theme is that there has been a decline of the classic democratic dialogue in our society and that it is having an unhealthy impact on our national life.

There is an old political truism, recognized by almost all of the practitioners of the art, that we never really know what we are like or what our fellow human beings are like until we have "a knife in our belly." In a certain sense, our society over the last twenty or thirty years has become one which has, and again I quote the politicians, "a knife in its belly."

We have lived for a very long time with all of our institutions working well. We are one of the only two nations in history, the other being England, that can truthfully claim to have a Constitution, and a group of political institutions which have enabled us to remain together and to handle our problems with a reasonable degree of efficiency for a very long period. The British began to develop their particular form of government as long ago as the thirteenth century. We started in 1789, and over the years we have had only one real breakdown—the Civil War. I am afraid that during that period we achieved a state of mind which encouraged us to take our institutions for granted. We assumed that what had been would always be, and that only occasionally would we have to tinker a bit with our governmental structures. In the past few years we have found that knife in our belly, and we have made the rather astounding discovery that we really do not understand our own institutions too well. We have become uncertain as to how they work and what to do about them, and we are not quite as confident about the future as we were twenty or thirty years ago.

We have lived through some astounding times. We have witnessed the burning of our cities during the riots in the ghettos. We have experienced "trashing" in our streets by

some of our young people. We have seen violent demonstrations by the "hard hats." And even those events, un-
settling as they were, are not quite as serious, in my judgment, as the nationwide feeling of apathy that is now so
widespread.

We have, for the moment, a certain type of calm. There
is no burning, no "trashing," no invasions of Wall Street
with monkey wrenches. But I cannot avoid the feeling
that this is a reflection of temporary exhaustion. Human
beings can only endure a limited amount of passion, and
we have not yet really recovered from the emotional or-
gies of the past few decades.

There is no mood of confidence. I think this is evident
in the fact that we are close to an election and there is no
real enthusiasm demonstrated for the upcoming national
campaign. When our people discuss politics, they are
much more interested in bond issues, road issues, and
school issues. Our Presidential candidates are wasting
their thunder on the desert air. I can detect among my
colleagues in the Democratic Party and my friends in the
Republican Party no genuine enthusiasm for any leader,
although it may develop further down the road.

This is very unusual in our history. I do not believe
that it is merely a temporary aberration—an accidental
set of circumstances that has followed a few wrong decisions by inadequate leaders. Even though there have
been plenty of wrong decisions and plenty of inadequate
leaders, the causes are far deeper. This is what I propose
to examine in the course of these lectures.

I begin with a point which seems very elementary, and yet I have discovered in talking to audiences in many places that it is a point usually ignored.

We have fallen into the habit of discussing our institutions and discussing our offices as though power were in the institutions themselves. We speak of the Presidency in terms of the "powers" of the Presidency. We speak of local politics in terms of the "powers" of the State House and the "powers" of City Hall. There is an odd confusion of shape and content in this phrase which I even find myself using if I am not very careful. It is misleading because in reality there is no power in any of those institutions. There is no power in the Presidency, there is no power in the governorship, there is no power in the mayoralty. Those offices are merely structures through which we, as a people, have determined that power shall be legitimately exercised.

When times are serene, when our society is united, when there are no deep divisions within our land, the distinction becomes unimportant. In such times, no one questions the source of power or challenges its reasonable exercise. People merely accept it for what it is without troubling themselves over abstruse and somewhat metaphysical questions of origin. When strains and tensions mount in our society, however, the distinction becomes vital because it goes directly to the heart of our problems. I do not believe there is any way in which we can see it more clearly than in our examination of the Presidency itself.

In the last forty years, our national life has been marked by many occasions when the office of the Presidency has suddenly found itself with diminished power. It has never been completely without power, because these things do not happen overnight. But there have been many instances in which the man occupying the Presidency did not have enough power to govern effectively.

I think the first time in my memory that it really happened on an important scale was in the early 1930s when Herbert Hoover, as President of the United States, suddenly discovered that most of the vaunted powers of the Presidency were meaningless. He had lost what political hold he had over the people: the country was in extremely bad economic shape; he was under very heavy criticism and was on the way to becoming the "Devil of the Depression." When the American people finally had an opportunity, they voted him out with a vindictiveness that bordered on the savage. Although I was very young at the time, I can still recall the conversations of older people who were absolutely certain that Mr. Hoover relished the misery of his countrymen. They were convinced that he had plunged us deliberately into the Depression and could take steps that would put people back to work if he so desired. In later years, it came as quite a shock to me, as a child of the Depression, to discover that the man was not the monster depicted by my elders. My research convinced me that he was a man of intelligence, a man of integrity, a man of compassion, and a

man who had ideas as to what to do. He had every quality but political power. Unfortunately, the missing ingre-
dient nullified all the others.

Without political power, the best any President can do
is to maintain a housekeeping operation that keeps our
government pinned together on a minimum level until it
is possible to elect a successor who has the confidence of
the people and who, therefore, can act.

When Franklin D. Roosevelt came into office, he had
that kind of public support. At the time we all thought
that it was the programs that emerged so miraculously
and so quickly in the first hundred days that brought
back our confidence and restored the economic health of
the nation. In retrospect, my thinking has changed. I am
not at all certain that the programs had much to do with
it. I think what did it was that Roosevelt had political
power and had it on a scale that had not been enjoyed
by any American President in decades. With that political
power, the office of the Presidency once again loomed as
a strong and usable instrument which could lead the
American people out of the gloom of the Depression; the
programs were almost irrelevant. Probably anything
would have worked in view of the man's political power.

We had our next really serious lapse in the early 50s
when once again the office was occupied by a President
without power—Harry S. Truman. Today Mr. Truman
has become a folk hero—a status I believe he deserves.
He was a man of unparalleled courage. He was an intelligent man and he was certainly an honest man. We appre-

ciate those qualities now and we have forgotten the fantastic amount of abuse that was heaped upon him. We have forgotten the Gallup polls which fell to 28 percent popularity. We have forgotten the anti-Truman feeling that arose when General MacArthur came back from Korea. I have vivid memories of standing among the crowds on Pennsylvania Avenue while MacArthur came down the street like a conquering hero with the populace ready to give him anything he asked—possibly even the reins of government. This was the one occasion of my life when I felt that my country was on the verge of a breakdown. Mr. Truman could not handle the situation no matter how great his courage and integrity, and no matter what the Constitution said about the office of the Presidency. The office had no political power and it was tottering. About the only thing that restored the American sense of balance was the genuine political skill of Senator Richard B. Russell of Georgia, who conducted very careful, slow, patient hearings on Asia. Gradually, given some time to think, the American people recovered their perspective.

We have had another situation in which we came dangerously close to a similar breakdown, and that was during the last two years of the regime of Lyndon Johnson. I do not believe that anybody who saw the 1968 Chicago Democratic Convention, or who was at all close to the situation in our military forces and the rapidly declining morale among the troops, could look upon the events as anything other than a loss of political power. It is possible, of course, to present statistical evidence to dispute this contention, but it is not very impressive. A few days ago I attended a Senate Judiciary Subcommittee hearing during which the Chairman recited a long list of bills passed by Congress after President Johnson had abdicated office. Supposedly, this was evidence that his announced intention to retire did not cost him political power. I do not consider bill passage an adequate test. The office of the Presidency is more than a launching pad for legislative recommendations. For that matter, it is more than just a clerical office. The role of the President is to lead the nation, and the office must fill two functions. One is to manage the affairs of the country and the other is to hold the nation together—to give the nation some unity, to set a moral tone, to inspire confidence among our citizens. During the last two years of the Johnson administration, as during the last two years of the Hoover and the Truman administrations, the Presidency was unable to fill that role. Fortunately, the time periods were relatively brief. We did not break down completely. But we were brought face to face with the question of how a nation can sustain itself when the people lack confidence in their leadership. We discovered that when a President loses his political power there is nothing we can do but grin and bear it. The nation, in varying degrees, must just go leaderless until the next opportunity to elect a replacement. We lack the flexibility which would permit us to switch to some alternative.

Let us take this one step further. Just what is it in our

society that has led to this particular phenomenon? Why do modern Presidents lose their political power so easily and find themselves so early out of step with the American people?

Generally speaking one would assume that the modern President in this decade of the 70s should be in a far better position to "communicate" than his predecessors. He has instruments available to him that very few previous Presidents even knew existed. He can call upon the television industry to turn over its networks to him anytime he wants them. He has high-speed wires that pass messages back and forth all around the earth. He can, if he wishes, set up a television studio in the White House, as Lyndon Johnson did, with cameras kept warm twenty-four hours a day. You would think the communication process would be far easier, but instead it suddenly seems to have become more difficult. There is a clear thread running through all varieties of dissent. It is a general feeling on the part of our people that they are outside of the mainstream of government and are led by men and women who are not paying any attention to them. The image of leadership among our citizens today is one of remote aloofness. The violence we have witnessed is an expression of this psychology—a desire to smash institutions which do not seem to respond to human desires. This does not bode well for the future. It can easily mean a series of one-term Presidents with an occasional two-term President elected because the opposition party of the moment is too flabby. This situation bears a suspicious resemblance to that which preceded the Civil War.

The remoteness of the Presidency was built into the Constitution by the founding fathers themselves. They obviously did not intend to create a President who was close to the people. The Constitutional Convention which met at Philadelphia had been sparked about a year earlier when John Jay wrote a letter to George Washington in which he identified the question before the Confederation as: "Should we have a King?" And there is very little doubt from the debate that took place and from the records of the Federalist Papers that the founding fathers thought of the President in terms of a king although not in terms of a dictator. Their intention was to hold the Chief Executive in check by restricting and limiting the powers of government itself. They divided those powers. They provided for an elected President who would be subject indirectly to the will of the voters every four years. Nevertheless, they did not consider it ideal that he be close to the people. Therefore, they invoked a number of devices to insure a large degree of separation, including the Electoral College, and a franchise so restrictive there were probably only about 30,000 effective voters in our first election out of a nation of three million. The remoteness did not matter in that era because the President handled few issues that impinged directly on the daily lives of the citizens. They thought of him as one who would make treaties and would manage whatever wars came long. It was the golden age of local government when citizens were more interested in the town council than in the federal establishment.

The inauguration of mass government ushered in a new era. At first it was welcome. The local establishments had lost their capacity to manage the affairs of American citizens and the relief from economic problems that could be afforded by a strong central force was exhilarating. But gradually things began to change. An office that was conceived as a monarchy began to look like a monarchy.

Today, even the external signs have appeared. For example, the last four Presidents have referred to themselves as "we." That was a phrase that bothered me very much as a child when I found an old novel in which a Russian czar called himself: "We, Nicholas, Czar of all the Russias." I can understand the phrase a bit better now that I have been in the White House. I do not think that Mr. Nixon was merely exercising a personality quirk when the White House guards suddenly burst forth in Ruritanian uniforms or when he inaugurated elaborate ceremonies of ruffles and flourishes upon the visit of a foreign ambassador to the White House. I do not mind ceremony; I rather like it. I only suggest that externals frequently reflect an underlying condition. In this instance, I believe it is the essentially monarchical character of the White House.

There is another aspect to the question of aloofness. It is obvious that a man who has reached the Presidency has reached the very top of the political profession. The summit is a peculiar place, especially when it is occupied by the highly aggressive psychology of a political animal. Very few men reach the top spot unless they have such a psychology. When they get there, they retain all of their ambitious desires to advance but find they have no further goals. There is nothing more that the people can grant a President. Therefore, it is only a matter of time until constituencies fade in his sight. The larger question becomes the reaction of history to his administration rather than the reaction of voters. The reaction of history—especially history that has yet to be written—is a poor guide to public policy. And there can be little doubt that the question of history has become obsessive with our Presidents. The rapid rise of Presidential libraries in recent years has taken on almost megalomaniac overtones. They began with a very simple act in which Mr. Hoover walked out of the White House with a few papers and later presented them to Stanford University. Then came the Roosevelt Library at Hyde Park, somewhat larger but still a relatively modest effort. Next there was the Truman Library, much better planned and a bit more ambitious in scope. It was followed by the Eisenhower Library and the Kennedy Library, each one bigger and bigger. The Lyndon B. Johnson Library in Austin now has some thirty million pieces of paper, which means that Mr. Nixon will probably shoot for at least forty million papers when he erects his edifice.

I suggest there is something unhealthy about a form of

government in which a man who is faced with day-to-day problems of government devotes so much energy to his image in the future. I doubt seriously whether these libraries will help historians. On the contrary, such repositories will probably compound their problems. I doubt even more seriously that the libraries reflect a genuine concern for future generations and the problems they will face. They smack far more of the Egyptian Pharaohs who sought immortality through the erection of stone pyramids.

I repeat that the trends toward aloofness from the great mass of our people have been inherent in the office of the Presidency from the beginning. The new factor which has been added over the last twenty to forty years is the rise of mass society and the rise of mass communications. This meant a shift in the perceptions of the Chief Executive. No matter how exalted his position in the earlier days, it was impossible for him to think of his nation in any terms other than a collection of people. In a mass society, however, people become statistics, and their leader finds himself dealing more and more with columns of figures.

I did not realize the full significance of this point when I was actually in the White House. At that time, I was busy defending the Press Office from both press and President. Many things went past me of which I had no consciousness until a later period when I had time for reflection. The most important was the tendency of all White House inhabitants to regard all issues, not in terms of people, but in terms of sheer masses of statistics that had a life of their own and bore little relevancy to human beings.

Let me illustrate. Of the various statistics that came into the White House, the most impressive were those which sought to prove the progress of pacification in Viet Nam. I should have known that there was something wrong with them, simply because of the progression. One week 35 percent of Viet Nam would be pacified, the next week 40, the next week 45, the next week 50 percent. The real world does not operate that smoothly. But I had a high degree of confidence in the method by which the figures were compiled. I knew that generally speaking people in the government do not lie. The method was quite good. It was based on a check of the villages from time to time. Such questions were asked as whether the head man slept in the village and how long since villagers had paid taxes to the Viet Cong. Such questions were legitimate and should have resulted in a true picture. It was not until sometime after I had left the White House that the truth suddenly hit me. I ran into an old friend who had been engaged in the pacification program and whom I had not seen in many years. We sat down and had a long talk and slowly a picture emerged.

First, this man was only able to visit the villages on his beat once a month for about two hours. Second, he spoke no Vietnamese. Third, he was a menace to all the inhabitants as long as he was in their village. I have been in undeveloped areas of South America enough to learn that primitive people have a faculty for reading an outsider's face and getting rid of him by telling him what he wants to hear. That was what was happening to my friend. The answers he was getting were coming from people who wanted him out of the way because his very presence made them a target for Viet Cong reprisal. His figures were consolidated with other figures all over the country. By the time the consolidations reached Washington, they appeared to be as substantial as the laws of the Medes and the Persians. Yet all they represented was this "long nose" standing in the middle of a Vietnamese village and trying to understand responses from an alien culture.

This example could be duplicated many times over because it goes to the heart of the problem of mass government. Politicians do not function effectively in such an atmosphere. The political personality is not made for the cold world of figures. The political world is one in which men excel because they are sensitive, because they can read each other's faces, because they can see the little rising signs of anger when they irritate others, and because they can understand the need to soften the harsh edges of the human personality. This is impossible when they come to rely solely upon computers and upon worldwide communications systems. They need to engage in adversary debate with equals or their sensitivity deteriorates. The President cannot have the kind of adversary relationship with other people that would enable him to put the computer system in proper perspective. He is a form of king and no one argues with a king. He is isolated from the moment he steps into the White House because everyone around him is his subordinate.

There are two ways to isolate a man. One is to lock him up in a padded cell and deprive him of human companionship. The other is simply to be certain that everybody in his vicinity is his servant. The two methods are equally effective.

There is a chain of circumstances and it is vicious. Power breeds isolation. Isolation leads to the capricious use of power. In turn, the capricious use of power breaks down the normal channels of communication between the leader and the people whom he leads. This ultimately means the deterioration of power and with it the capacity to sustain unity in our society. This is the problem we face today.

I am going to explore this further in future remarks. For the time being, I open the floor for questions. Who wants to start off?

QUESTION:    In the situation that you have described, is it possible that the military would take over as Presidential power declines?

REEDY:    No, not at that particular point. The situation that you are raising I do not believe is upon us yet. My own reading of our military corps and those men that I have seen in high positions is that the tradition of civilian control is still so strong that we are not near any military coup. I think at the moment what we have to fear are these periods of a breakdown in Presidential power where he loses his capacity to lead. Should we fail to solve the overall problem of sustaining the consensus for our elected leaders, then the temptation will eventually arise for a military coup after which leadership would be sustained by armed force.

QUESTION: I am not quite clear on what you mean by a President who has political power. Is that the same thing as saying a President who has charismatic leadership quality?

REEDY: No, charismatic leadership is a part of it. But by political power, I mean all of the highly complicated processes of persuasion in a democratic society. Basically the political processes are substitutes for guns and clubs. Charismatic leadership is one of the most important elements. But there are other important elements such as force of habit on the part of the electorate, the political machinery the leader has built up over the years, the confidence that people have in him. It never breaks down all in one fell swoop unless there is an extreme situation such as the one that faced the Czar of All the Russias in 1917. At one point in time he had the greatest amount of formal power of any potentate in the world. Five minutes later he was a stumblebum out of work and getting ready to face a firing squad. In the United States, I believe we have a system that is more enduring and that cannot collapse all at once. It goes by degrees and it has yet to hit bottom. Even Harry Truman at his lowest ebb still had enough residues of power left to keep the country going on a housekeeping basis.

QUESTION:    Do you think that the fact that we elect the Congress every second year and that at certain times in the history of some of the Presidents the Congress has changed from supporting him politically to a majority against him is a mitigating circumstance or does that make it worse for him?

REEDY:    I actually think it's a mitigating circumstance. After a man has been in the White House for a few months, his point of

view starts changing very rapidly. He
finds himself leading a style of life that it
is very easy to become accustomed to.
When a Presidential family first enters the
White House, the members feel as though
they are living in a museum. Every time
they turn around they fear they are
going to smash a $100,000 vase or some
priceless heirloom. After all, this property belongs to the people. After a while,
however, they start thinking that this is a
normal way of life. The consciousness of
royalty sets in. I believe the mid-term
election, where Presidents usually get a
jolt, is probably a healthy force to bring
them a little way back down to earth. Of
course, the reason a President's political
party usually loses in the mid-term election is that it picked up more seats than
it was entitled to when it won the Presidency. The mere fact that a winning
President is on top of the ticket usually
brings in a number of Congressmen
from districts that are not normally dedi-
cated to his party. I believe the mid-term
jolt is not a protest against the President
quite as much as it is a return to normal
voting patterns. But Presidents always
interpret it as a jolt and this gives them a
degree of humility. I think one of the

reasons, by the way, that Mr. Nixon did not lose so heavily in this last mid-term election is that for the first time in history a President came in and didn't bring many Congressmen with him.

QUESTION: Isn't every official apt to get far away from the people he is supposed to serve?

REEDY: You must begin with the proposition that any amount of rising in life isolates a man to some degree. Everytime we step up the ladder people fall away from us just another step or two more. The difference between the Presidency and others is that the Presidency is about as close to total estrangement as one can get in the modern world. The only time he ever meets a peer is during the rare visit of some foreign potentate, and since there are so few countries today that have the resources and power of the United States, most of the potentates who visit the United States feel a bit diffident.

QUESTION: You find that the office of the President leads to a certain kind of isolation, yet what accounts for the fact that Roosevelt held two press conferences a week and our latest President no more frequently than one a month. Why is this thing working the other way? What is the cause of this decline?

REEDY: There is a basic difference in temperament between the two, but I think the more important thing is that Roosevelt was President during a period of rising confidence and rising expectations and he was a very buoyant man and matched the mood of the country. He was extremely extroverted; he loved back-and-forth exchanges with the press. Those are the only Presidential press conferences that I have ever enjoyed. I covered a few of them as a young man and it was marvelous for about ten of us to be standing around that desk with the President trying to catch us in any little trap he could. Of course, we were trying to catch him in a few too. But since then, so many of the rising expectations have been dashed. The character of the times have changed, and with it, the character of our political leaders. I think to some extent that our political leaders are reflecting our own moods. You know, Gary Wills in his book *Nixon Agonistes* says that it is a mistake to believe that the election process always produces the best man for the job, but it always produces an appropriate man for the times. People are not as confident today as they were forty years ago and our Presidents reflect this change in mood. Another factor is that since Roosevelt we have developed what we regard as a science of communication, a science of motivation. There are techniques which I believe are quite valid in certain fields of business and industry, but which, I think, hamper rather than accelerate the political process. Political leaders are quite obsessed with these techniques and believe that when they meet the press today they must put on a production which takes considerable time to prepare. Roosevelt merely called in the press and answered their questions.

*QUESTION:*    When the President begins to feel the political power slipping away from him, does he recognize this and what tactics does he take to regain it?

*REEDY:*    In the last two examples, the Presidents have tried to make up for it with an out-

pouring of statements and legislative re-
quests, and a more aggressive stance,
which in turn made them slip more. One
of the very dreary memories to me in the
closing days of Harry Truman were
these continual laundry lists of bills he
kept sending up to the Congress. He'd
send up forty or fifty measures, many of
which were quite admirable, but none of
which had the slightest chance of passage. The same thing happened with
Lyndon Johnson. His staff began to
shovel bills into the legislative hopper.

*QUESTION:*     John Gardner has expressed in regard to
the quality of our institutions, political
and legal, the desire to have them
changed or modified in certain ways so
they are more reflective of people's
views. I am aware of his interest in Congress and in the courts, but has he said
anything about the Presidency itself?

*REEDY:*     Not about the Presidency, no. He has de-
voted himself to a much greater extent
to the executive agencies and in a sense I
think he is right. The organization of the
Presidency is irrelevant to the overall
problem. I do not care how the Presi-

dency is organized; it is going to react the same way, as long as certain power relationships remain unchanged. It is amazing the extent to which political power realities override organizational forms. For instance, many years ago they set up the National Security Council to guarantee that the President would get adversary debate among experts on highly important matters. I sat in many meetings of the National Security Council, which was called faithfully about every other week. We had some marvelous performances and it was impossible to escape the feeling that everything was scripted. Nobody ever got mad at anybody; no fists were pounded on the table; nobody suggested that somebody else commit a biological improbability. This was because the real work was done at Tuesday lunches with the Secretary of State and the Secretary of Defense and the Chief of the CIA. The Presidency is a political institution and it is a mistake to expect that organizational change will ever make much difference in a political institution. There is one point where I disagree with Mr. Gardner. I quite agree with him on what has to be done in many of the executive offices but I do not believe reorganization of Congress makes much difference. I went through one of them as a newspaperman back in 1946 when they made a tremendous effort known as the LaFollette-Monroney Act. There were 55 House committees as I recall and 32 Senate committees, and they were reorganized and streamlined down to about 28 House committees, 17 Senate committees, and at least 100 subcommittees, each complete with chairman, stationery, and staff. When dealing with political institutions, technical reorganization is just meaningless.

QUESTION: If it is true that the Presidency holds the power only at the will of the people, how do you explain the fact that President Nixon was elected by barely 51 percent of the vote and has still been able to make sweeping changes and form the government in his own image after coming in with so little?

REEDY: You are speaking in terms of votes and I am speaking in terms of political power. They are two different things. The vote is basically the formal authorization by which a man comes to office. Political power is the man's ability to get people to do what he wants them to do. There are all sorts of reasons why a man might have only 51 percent of the votes, or even less, and still be able to make some rather sweeping changes. While it is true that nothing loses like losing, nothing wins like winning. Many Presidents have found their following has increased enormously the day after election.

*QUESTION:*   What influence do you think the two-term limitation has?

*REEDY:*   I think it is a terrible thing. The only thing that's worse than the two-term limitation is the one six-year limitation. I have spent quite a bit of time in South America and one of the most perfect examples that I have seen of the workings of Presidential term limitations was in Chile. I was there a few years ago and there is absolutely no question that there was only one political leader in the country who could get a majority in an election, and that was Eduardo Frei. He had the political institutions of the country pretty much in his corner. But he couldn't succeed himself under the Chilean Constitution which provides for one six-year term. The result is that they elected Allende by 36½ percent of the vote and they are stuck with him for six years. I believe they are going to have real trouble because Allende does not have much support in depth in the country. Any absolute limit on the length of time a man can serve is an invitation to trouble. Generally speaking, I think most Presidents would only serve two terms anyway. It is an exhausting job, not because of the work involved but because of the crushing weight of decisions.

QUESTION: Are you suggesting that Lyndon Johnson in that famous March speech saw that he was indeed slipping and thus bowed out, or can—question two—could he have won had he not bowed out?

REEDY: His re-election would have been doubtful but I think he has convinced himself that he would have won, which is the normal thing to be expected. When you are dealing with Lyndon Johnson you are dealing with a very complex man. I was very close to him for many years, I think as close as anybody, and I still find myself trying to penetrate certain enigmas and trying to determine what he was really like. I have a feeling, however, that the explanation he gave at the time was the valid one, and because he had given a lot of other explanations on other things, I think people simply didn't believe it. I believe at that point he really wanted to get a Conference with the North Vietnamese. He was correct in thinking that he wasn't going to get that Conference if he were a candidate for re-election. That would look just like a political ploy. And that is one time when I think he should really be taken at face value.

QUESTION:    You speak as if these men, both Johnson and Truman, were unable to size up the political situation in terms of effectiveness when they were in office. They were notably good men before. I don't understand the change.

REEDY:    Trying to figure it out is what led to my book. I think that Lyndon Johnson as a Senate leader was one of the ablest and

most subtle and strongest political leaders of our times. He did a fantastic job
of taking a Democratic Party that was
shattered and reuniting it. I can recall in
the early days when I was working for
him and he was the Senate Democratic
leader; we didn't dare let two Democrats
get into the same room together. They
would gouge each other's eyes out. Inside of a year, he had them voting together; inside of two years he had a
strong party that had a strong national
image and I think it was that national
image that won the Congress back for
us. He certainly did not demonstrate that
political perspicacity in the White House.
In trying to understand why, I thought
back to his days as the Majority Leader.
He would enter the building in the
morning, head for his office, and there
would be Allen Ellender waiting on the
front doorstep. Allen Ellender was quite
a forceful character and very conservative. He would be blazing with complaints that the leadership was too liberal. Lyndon Johnson would soothe him
down and in would come Wayne Morse
with complaints that the leadership was
too conservative. The whole day was

like that—bing! bing! bing! At the end of the day, Lyndon Johnson was in very close touch with political reality. When he entered the White House all that ended. I can recall an occasion about six or seven months after I had left the White House, when I met Senator Russell at a party in Washington. I said to him: "Senator, do things look as bad as I think they do?" and he said "Yes they do, George." And I said, "Senator you used to be quite effective in talking to the President. Why don't you make a trip down to the White House and have a heart-to-heart talk." And his response was, "George, I can't talk to a President the way I can talk to a Senator." And this to me was the key. There *is* a difference in status which separates the President from his peers because if a United States Senator is not the peer of a President, who is? Politicians need peers and without them they become remote from reality.

QUESTION:    Can't the President take some initiative to break that boundary?

REEDY:    Kennedy tried on many occasions. His efforts became common gossip throughout

Washington. Very minor desk officers from the State Department and the Pentagon would be startled to pick up the telephone and hear at the other end a voice saying: "This is President Kennedy." He would then try to get an honest evaluation. It was not a very successful effort. People do not take a king very seriously when he asks them to unbend. There have been too many lessons in history as to what happened to those who complied. Everybody recalls Mao Tsetung saying: "Let a hundred flowers bloom." Remember what happened to those flowers when they bloomed? They had their heads chopped off. Furthermore, people become tongue-tied when they are in the presence of a President. In 1964 Barry Goldwater and George Wallace were galloping around the country and accusing Lyndon Johnson of every crime from mopery on the highways to carrying concealed ideas. Both acted as though they just wanted to get into that White House and get their hands on Johnson so they could tell him some truths. Well, they both had to come into the White House during that campaign for some unimportant reasons which I have

forgotten. They were the mildest, meek-
est Casper Milquetoasts I've ever seen
in my life. Those men were not afraid of
Lyndon Johnson. It was the President
who overawed them.

QUESTION:    What about the newspapers? Won't they
play a role in presenting the President
with adversary criticism? Doesn't he get
some unvarnished truth from them?

REEDY:    The problem is that the press comes to the
President in written form. He knows that
stories are written, edited, put in print,
and that a parallel process goes on in
television. Therefore, it is very simple
for a President to convince himself that
this is just a conspiracy—of the eastern
press, the liberal establishment, the
southern press, the western press. Everybody around him will assure him that
this is the case. The White House in rela-
tion to the press regards itself as a belea-
guered fortress. And this is true of all
the assistants. I finally got to a point
where I hated to go down to the mess
for lunch because all I would hear would
be a lot of gripes and a lot of squawks
from all the other assistants on the no-

good press, when usually they were talking about matters where I thought the
press was right. A man can always de-
cide that something is a conspiracy if
there is a certain impersonal element between him and the source. What he can't
label as a conspiracy is a conversation
with a man face to face.

QUESTION:    Actually do you think we would be better off without the office of the President
at all or a committee type of Executive
Office?

REEDY:    You cannot have a committee type of
government because nothing would be
done, and you can't abolish the job because there must be some embodiment
of legitimacy and continuity. The problem is to somehow establish peers for the
President. I believe we must work this
out within the system we have now.

# CHAPTER 2

## THE AUTOMATED
## POLITICAL DIALOGUE

WHAT I WANT to do now is to move into the next stage of what has happened to us over the last forty or fifty years and what forces have brought us to the position where somehow the dialogue between people—the type of communication that should exist between political leaders and the people who are being led —has broken down. The fact that it has broken down is not the sort of thing that can be measured, quantified, viewed through some kind of a spectroscope with numerical qualities assigned to the various shades. Unfortunately, we live in an age of quantification, and I think one of our greatest problems in trying to understand the world around us is that the most important aspect of it, the most important element, that thing which will determine whether we do survive as a free people or whether we go into some other type of society cannot be quantified. It is the human brain rather than the computer that must answer the'basic question of why our political leadership has failed.

I think it might be well, for a moment, to go back and survey the situation of forty or fifty years ago. It was not a wonderful world. There were many, many problems. And it was far different from the world that exists today. I know I find it very difficult in talking to my own sons to try to convey to them some flavor of the 20s, some concept of this period of our national existence, when I myself was only a small boy—but nevertheless a small boy who was acutely aware of the political currents around me.

As the son of a newspaperman, I very early fell in love with the political process. I roamed Chicago with my father who was determined that I would not be a newspaperman. Somehow he thought the way to do it was to take me with him on his beat during my summer vacations while he would stand the night trick at the Chicago City Detective Bureau and have me visit the police stations, the various ward offices, and all of the institutions and people that were so much a part of his routine. After that kind of experience, it was futile for him to try to pressure me to go into the study of law. I had become too enchanted with the political life of this tremendous city.

I think I also recognized early that I did not have the

temperament to become the kind of politician who would run for office. I did not have the necessary "instinct for the jugular" which I think is essential to any political leader. But the process itself appealed to me as one of the most absorbing and one of the most fascinating of all human relationships.

Chicago in those days was an exciting city. A boy with a reasonable amount of sensitivity and a reasonable amount of curiosity could travel throughout the whole world. He could readily avail himself of all the experiences of Marco Polo. There were the rich, bubbly smells of peppers and tomatoes in the Italian section; the holidays in the Czechoslovakian section, where the Sokols engaged in gymnastics; the delights of Kosciusko Day in Humboldt Park where fiery orators praised the glorious victories of John Sobieski while gaily clad matrons at makeshift stands sold glasses of slivovitz thoughtfully labeled "plum juice" in deference to the laws of Prohibition; the *Gemütlichkeit* of the German Turnvereins where stout burgers sang "Du, Du, Liegst Mir im Herzen" over seidels of forbidden beer and heaping mounds of sauerkraut and knockwurst. It was a city of great diversity, with all of the ethnic neighborhoods very carefully separated geographically and all of them bound together with equal care by a political machine.

The politics, in many respects, were sordid, resting upon paving contracts, thievery, banality, thuggery and outright defiance of the "noble experiment" of Prohibition.

But there was another aspect to it, a quality that we

should have retained in one form or another: it was very human. It is rather difficult for us to understand, in this age of polarization when we establish formal political quotas based on sex, skin color, economic status and age levels, the simple but effective mechanisms by which our cities in those days were kept relatively serene. Basically the machines rested upon the ward leader and the precinct captain. What they had done was to set up in an extremely pragmatic form and upon a crassly commercial basis a system which gave the average member of the ghetto and the average representative of the various nationality groups a feeling that he was at one end of a direct pipeline to City Hall.

This was vital, because it was still the age of the immigrant. If you were a poor Hungarian or a poor Pole or a poor Czech or a poor mick or a poor anyone else just arrived from the old country, you were a stranger in an alien land. The discrimination in those days was not only rife; it was open and avowed to an extent that is almost unbelievable to the modern generation. It was common on the vaudeville stage of the Palace Theater to have Jewish comedians who made a living year after year after year on gags that had no more wit to them than the Gentile belief that poor Cohen yearned to eat ham but dared to do so only when the Rabbi's back was turned. There was a comic strip with tremendous readership in the United States in which the sole humor was the relationship between Jiggs, an Irish hod carrier who had made some money, and his wife Maggie, who wanted to break into society. Poor Jiggs had no sympathy for the endeavor and was constantly sneaking out to Dinty Moore's for a plate of corned beef and cabbage in order to escape Maggie's efforts to drag him to the opera. The pathos of the situation—the futile effort to attain the status to which Jiggs was entitled by his economic success —eluded most of the readers. It was taken for granted that a Negro (openly called a "spade") was interested only in eating tremendous quantities of watermelon and in avoiding all of the work that he possibly could. And I can still remember the time when we shared a two-apartment house with a family named Robleski whose two young daughters had rather good secretarial jobs in a law office in the Loop. They held those jobs because they had dropped the "ski" from their names and had been hired as Roble. If their employers had learned that they were really "Robleski," they would have been fired the next day.

Within this milieu the immigrant was faced with tremendous problems. But he did have one institution on his side. He had his precinct captain and his ward leader. And through them he could make himself felt all the way to City Hall. It was really a rather dignified sort of arrangement when you look at it in retrospect. He did not have to go to some petty official and fill out a form specifying the number of people in the family; whether the family had bought a television set; whether he was using contraceptives; how much of the family income was spent upon milk and how much upon bread or whether they were paying proper attention to the health of their children. It was very simple. On Thanksgiving, the precinct captain would show up with a turkey and at Christmas with a ton of coal; in the winter he would pass out slips that meant a job shoveling snow, and in the spring slips that led to a job at Riverview Park. The only thing the immigrant was required to offer in return for all these favors was his vote. It was an open and aboveboard transaction. Neither the donor nor the donee was embarrassed. They merely shook hands and the deal was consummated.

I do not want anyone to assume that I am sentimental about that age. It meant horrible graft, corruption in our cities, the famous "million dollar bridle path" in the Sanitary District (a county governmental unit), towns such as Burnham and Stickney that were openly controlled by gangsters who made their living by peddling booze. But there was one thing in that system that was valuable. In an era when people were oriented primarily toward City Hall—when Washington was a remote place that one only thought about during wartime—the average citizen, even the immigrant at the bottom of the ladder, felt that he had a direct voice within his government and a direct form of participation.

I think it may be instructive to add one footnote. In those years the only serious riot that broke out in the city of Chicago involved the one group of people that was *not* included within this political system—the Blacks. They were still outside the pale and were not part of the operations of the city machines. "Big Bill" Thompson, the man who was actually elected Mayor of Chicago on the platform that he was going to take the first boat to England and "punch King George in the snoot," did make some speeches in an appeal for the Black vote. But speeches were his only gift to the Afro-Americans who had swarmed into the South Side in a search for jobs and dignity. It was many years later that they succeeded in obtaining a modicum of recognition by erecting their own political power structure.

Again, I repeat that I am not advocating the tawdry political system of the twenties and I am not an admirer of it. But I think it affords us one lesson we should bear in mind. To keep some form of order in society, there must be a feeling that the government is something in which the average person, the "poor Joe" in the street, is directly involved, and that he is not just somebody who is being ruled, but a citizen who can exercise certain levers of power.

What happened to those levers of power? What was it that over a period of a few decades transformed us from a nation oriented primarily toward the local machine to a nation oriented toward the national machine, from a nation in which citizens did have this sense of participation to a nation in which they felt remote from government?

Of course, the most important thing was that this local structure, the city machine, simply could not stand up against the harsh impact of the Depression. Within months after the stock market crashed, Chicago was unable to pay its schoolteachers, its policemen, and its firemen. I can still recall the worried faces of some of my teachers when they came to our apartment with scrip that Chicago was issuing in lieu of salaries. They were trying to persuade my parents to buy it at a discount, and it was terribly difficult to tell them we did not have any money either and were hoping we could sell something too. Out of this crisis began the age of mass government.

The Republicans and the Conservatives, very foolishly at that time, tried to stop the centralization of government and it could not be stopped because the national catastrophe was so sweeping that cities and states were helpless to deal with it. It required massive amounts of money. It required massive exercise of leadership to put this nation back on its feet. There was a bewildering succession of alphabetical agencies—the WPA, the PWA, the NYA (without which I could never have gotten through college), the Civilian Conservation Corps, and all of the organizations through which the federal government, for the first time in history, asserted its obligation to step in and help people out when the going was rough. That could not have been reversed. It was a process of history, and the outpouring of gratitude and warmth toward Franklin Delano Roosevelt was such that he became an absolutely invincible leader. We did not realize that these steps, though necessary, were taken at a price, and the price was the establishment of mass government.

To transfer the focus of government from the local area—from the city, from the county, even from the State House—to Washington, D.C., entails the establishment of controls that have become very much a part of our age. Federal money does not go out from the Treasury without some effort on the part of the federal government to assure that the funds are spent wisely and effectively. There must be means of checking; there must be machinery that determines what the local officials are doing with the funds; and there must be agents to follow up and make certain that the money is going where it is really supposed to go. And with that comes not only the necessity for mass controls but also mass communications.

Lewis Mumford in his remarkable book *The Myth of the Machine* compares the present era with that of pyramid building in Egypt, when the pharaohs, one after another, built larger and larger and larger pyramids which absorbed all of the surplus energy of Egypt and ultimately brought collapse to their whole system. It simply could not bear the weight of this tremendously wasteful activity. I think that in a sense his comparison of that age with our age does have much validity, particularly in light of the social structures we have built in the past forty years. We have gone from the highly pluralistic society of our ancestors—not completely and perhaps not even three-quarters of the way but still a considerable distance—to a pyramidal structure in which leadership is exercised through institutions which assume that power comes down from the top rather than rises from the bottom. And what happens to such a society? Since it exercises mass controls, since it depends upon mass communication, the next step is to develop a "science" of mass manipulation.

The process began in a rather simple way with the publicity agents, such as the advance men for Ringling Brothers Barnum and Bailey or the famous Ivy Lee who managed to promote September Morn into a place of honor on almost every middle-class American wall by hiring small schoolchildren to stand outside a shop window and snicker and point at the picture while Anthony Comstock passed by. Then came the public relations firms, which grew larger and larger as they developed a whole new vocabulary of public relations and motivational techniques. Eventually this movement spread to the political realm itself. The political leaders were dealing with the techniques of mass communication, and the temptation to seek out and exercise what they regarded as the levers of public opinion was overwhelming. Over the years a basic difference of tone entered our political dialogue. There was a time when I found politicians to be fascinating people. I gloried in their conversation. I could sit and listen to them talk for hours. What they were discussing was the substance of politics, and the substance of politics is people—their passions and their moods. Today a session with a group of political leaders is boring. They no longer discuss people or the political process. Instead, their conversation is entirely about some weird, occult discipline known as PR. Should they continue along this path, and there is no evidence they will change, the high priests of our civilization will soon be the public relations men. The difficulty is that PR, when adopted on a broad and massive basis by the political leaders of our land, introduces into our society a distinct note of unreality—a feeling that something is missing from the ordinary dialogue.

Let me illustrate. The problem with all public relations techniques, motivational research and concepts of manipulating human behavior, is that as rapidly as the techniques become known, they become ineffective. If they become known at all, they must be known to more than a few people and if they are known to more than a few people, they quickly become a subject of common conversation, and if they become a subject of common conversation, the people feel they are being sold a bill of goods. There was an excellent example of this process in the first few months after President Nixon took office. Day after day I saw story after story of his assistants congratulating themselves upon the excellence of President Nixon's public relations techniques. Well, the obvious answer is that when people start talking about a man's public relations techniques, he does not have any. If he is really relating to the public and really communicating effectively and successfully, no one is going to think in terms of public relations techniques. They are going to think instead of what he has said, of what he is trying to do, of the goals he is trying to achieve.

There is another problem with mass communications, and it is a very serious problem. What must be done is to standardize such communications, and the moment standardization sets in words take on a different form. They lose their original meaning, and the necessity of interpreting them breeds cynicism. I can well recall this from my college days when I roomed with a Russian boy from Harbin, Manchuria. His parents were white Russian so I had to discount in part his opinion of the Bolshevik government. But he had one story which I believed and which I think sheds considerable light on the whole question of the modern mass manipulative techniques which are driving us so far from our leaders. He said that if a Soviet citizen were to pick up a copy of *Pravda* and see on the front page a story extolling cabbage—cabbage has vitamins A to Z, cabbage will make the hair curly, cabbage is a deodorant, cabbage will make the eyes blue, cabbage will increase sexual virility—the Russian would say to himself: "Ah ha! The wheat crop has failed again."

Years later I had another experience, something I could observe very directly. During World War II, when I was stationed in the Pacific with the 20th Air Force, our best entertainment before the armed forces put a radio station in Saipan, was the English language broadcasts of Tokyo Rose from Japan. They were not very good. She had some old records—I believe her most up-to-date number was "Tiger Rag." Nevertheless it was better than just sitting around playing poker while pedigreed rats, descended from those on Magellan's ships, ran across our legs in the coral boondocks of northern Guam. Between musical numbers, she would broadcast news bulletins which presented the following picture: On Monday, the Japanese Navy would meet the American Navy and sink it off the Philippines; on Tuesday, the Japanese Navy would meet the American Navy and sink it off Formosa; on Wednesday, the Japanese Navy would meet the American Navy and sink it off the Marianas; on Thursday, the American fleet would be sunk off the Bonins and on Friday off Okinawa. All of this came as a considerable surprise to our own Navy, which was desperately hoping it could find a Japanese ship somewhere because our sailors needed some target practice. We listened and thought: "Those poor devils! They are being pounded; they have lost the War; and they think they are winning." When we entered Japan, we discovered that the Japanese people had not been fooled in the slightest. They had figured out that each one of those Japanese naval "victories" had brought the American fleet 500 miles closer to Japan.

There is a rather important lesson in these stories. We should be skeptical of the capacity of word manipulators to delude people for any great length of time, or even mislead them, as long as the events described by those words bear some relevancy to the things they are experiencing in their daily lives. I think it might be possible to fool the average American about Afghanistan; I doubt if it would be possible to fool the average American about Viet Nam. We just have had too many of our men in that country. I think it might be possible to fool the average American about the state of our scientific research on quasars or the black holes in the universe; I doubt if it would be possible to delude them too much (although they can be confused) about the state of the food they eat, or the chemicals that are being used, or the nutrition their children can expect to get.

But despite the rather demonstrable fact, in my judgment, that in the field of politics the motivational techniques and the public relations ploys are not working, our political leaders are relying more and more on them. Since we are in the age of the mass society, politicians feel they must use these methods which come to them so highly commended and that they must express themselves through approved techniques which have been "tested" and which have acquired the sanctity of quantification. I believe the harder they try, in a very important sense, the further away they drive themselves from the average American.

Some very peculiar things are happening to our language. We have all become inured to the political nonspeech. We have all become inured to the political nonthought. The result is that we have also reached a point where we find some very important words being eliminated from our vocabularies. Consider, for example, "progressive," "creative," "exciting," "new." Does anyone here ascribe a meaning to them today? They have become mere passwords and countersigns so that mediocrities can recognize each other. What has really happened to us is that we have been deprived of our words of excellence and our words of passion. We are drowning in a high tide of meaningless speeches—such as those in the Rose Garden which became known among the White House staff as "Rose Garden rubbish." What happens, and I think this is not fully understood, is that when words of excellence and words of passion are eliminated from the language by overuse and by applying them to flawed objects, our citizens become distrustful of all forms of communication. There is little mystery in the desire of our young people to speak with a new tongue.

While my sons were still living with the family, I had a marvelous time following the language of the younger generation. I regret the fact that it is no longer possible now that they have both moved on—one to graduate school and the other to undergraduate school—and are at home very little. I miss the days when I learned that "tough" really meant inspiring, that "cool" really meant beautiful, and that "cube" was a description of their father whom they regarded as square squared. There was a certain delight in the unexpected uses of the words, and I believe I understand their motivation. They were simply trying to restore meaning to the English language.

In this age of mass communication, so much has been invested in tremendous networks, in electronics, in equipment, in commentators, that executives are afraid to make enemies because enemies might imperil economic existence. This means that they tend to avoid controversy, which means they must avoid excellence. Any thought worth expressing necessarily provokes opposition. Therefore, we continue an empty dialogue which has less and less meaning for the American people.

When I first read George Orwell's *1984*, it seemed incredible that there could be a world in which war was called peace, tyranny was called justice, and hate was called love. I have discovered now that there is such a world. There was only one thing wrong with Orwell's prognostication: people resist such a world with greater intensity than he predicted. They do not respond to manipulation. They merely draw into their shells and the result is not a healthy one for our society. We have broken down not only the methods by which people once had direct access to their leaders but also the language through which they communicated with those leaders. I am afraid we are going to pay a heavy price.

At this point I would like to throw the floor open for questions because this is a predicate for my next and final lecture. Who wants to start off?


*QUESTION:*    I wonder if you agree that part of the process of the breakdown in communication is due to our transformation from a rural to an urban society. This may be even more important than the factors which you cited because there were no city machines in the rural areas.

*REEDY:* I think that it should be pointed out that in the rural areas you also had the same direct connection between the people and their county governments.

*QUESTION:* You said that you think that the American public doesn't buy this gobbledy-gook which the political leadership is throwing at us. Do you believe a fresh, new spirit can get up and speak the truth and get elected?

*REEDY:* I am absolutely convinced of it. One of the strange things, in looking back over the many years that I have spent in Washington, is that for a long time I had difficulty understanding the great popularity of Robert A. Taft. There was a man who not only was against most of the things I stood for, but also, I thought, was out of step with the great current of the American people. But he had one important quality. He would not stand for any flap-doodle. It was wonderful to hear Bob Taft suddenly stand up on the Senate floor and say: "The distinguished

Senator is speaking nonsense. The bill on the floor is HR 347 and the Senator is obviously under the misimpression that we are considering S 561." And the newspapermen, few of whom were in agreement with Taft, really had a kind of love for him.

I have a feeling that the chain of manipulation must be broken somehow. I think our leaders have become so completely obsessed with a concept of public relations techniques which have proven successful in the commercial field, but which bear little or no relevancy to the political field, that they have forgotten the political realities. There is no doubt in my mind that the public is hungry for a breath of fresh air, for people who will talk to them like adults.

*QUESTION:*   If these techniques are successful in the commercial field, which personally I cannot understand, why are they not successful in the political field?

*REEDY:*   Because the techniques have been worked out on the basis of certain assumptions that apply in the commercial field and not in politics. For instance, if a man wants to apply public relations techniques to the sale of soap, he can start with the assumption that there are only three or four brands of soap and the consumer's choice is relatively limited. The soaps are all going to do the job of hand-washing just about the same way. Therefore, the public will probably choose on the basis of the advertising because there is no other standard for selection. This is not true in the political field where people usually have a real choice. The other assumption basic to the application of commercial public relations is that the client can be put on stage when it is advantageous and taken off stage when circumstances warrant. A PR representative can plan his advertising, can plan his mail campaign, and can move at a time of his own choice. But in the political world there are all sorts of inconvenient events that disrupt planning. If a bomb drops somewhere in the world, obviously the President of the United States must be available to react. If there is a vote on the Senate floor, a Senator must show up and vote no matter how strategically inconvenient it may be. But I think ultimately the difference goes back to the fact that in the commodities field you do have a limitation of choice which you do not have in the political field. In the political field you have a process that eventually narrows down to a limitation of choice, yes, but along the way there are plenty of opportunities for the people to winnow things out, and while I think public relations techniques will frequently work the first time around, I just don't think that they win in the long run.

QUESTION: I was wondering about the technique of polls as a means of mass communication and I have often wondered whether they were effective from a political point of view. If Rockefeller takes a poll, he certainly advertises it if he thinks it looks good, and then you never know whether to believe it.

REEDY: I think what happens is that politicians use the polls as a weapon, as an instrument of political warfare. And they believe them when the polls are running in their favor, and when the polls aren't running in their favor, they go out and get a new set. But when it comes to the practical day-to-day work, you will find that they discard them very rapidly. One of my earliest experiences was in working with the Senate Preparedness Subcommittee. We were trying to put through Congress a bill for universal military training. It seemed that it should be a very easy thing because all of the polls showed an overwhelming percentage of the American people were for universal military training. I believe Gallup even had one that went as high as 90 percent or some such fantastic figure. Yet we discovered that we could not persuade a Senate majority or a House majority to vote for universal military training. Too many members regarded the 80 or 90 percent figure as a response from people who did not feel intensely about the issue. What concerned them was the opposition response which they felt came from people who were not indifferent to it. To vote for universal military training would not *assure* a legislator one vote of that 80 or 90 percent but it was certainly going to lose forever and for all time to come the other twenty or ten. And until the polls can really measure intensity of feeling—and I doubt very

much if they ever will be able to do that
—I am skeptical.

*QUESTION:*    Would you comment on the development
of public relations between the period of
Roosevelt and Nixon.

*REEDY:*    Actually the public relations syndrome
didn't begin in a professional sense until
some time after Mr. Roosevelt left office.
There were in those days a number of
people who were actually practicing in-
formal public relations and I think they
were the men who sold the politicians on
it. I can recall many political leaders
who were fully convinced that Charley
Michaelson of the Democratic National
Committee staff was the most potent
weapon that Roosevelt had. Even then I
was somewhat skeptical, because Charley was merely producing slick slogans. I
have always doubted very much whether
such slogans really elected Roosevelt. I
don't think the American people elected
Roosevelt time after time after time because they wanted him to eliminate the
"princes of privilege" and the "malefactors of great wealth." I believe they just
thought that he was enacting programs

that were putting people back to work. But the legend of Charley Michaelson lived on in Washington. Finally, sometime in the 40s came the rise of a number of firms that arranged a "talk-a-thon" in storefront windows and of men who would package whole campaigns such as the campaign for John Marshall Butler against Millard Tydings in which everything turned on a radio slogan "Be for Butler, Be for Butler, Be for Butler." Butler was elected, which convinced everyone that the campaign had worked. I myself think the truth was that Mr. Tydings had been in office for about thirty years and had accumulated so many enemies that Butler would have beaten him that year if he had just stayed home.

Nevertheless, no matter how questionable the efficacy of public relations techniques in politics, they dominate the Washington scene today. I do not know of a single Senator, and I know of very few House members, who is without a Press Relations man. When I first started to cover the Hill as a newspaperman, there was no such thing as a Press Relations man in either House of Congress.

Sometimes, in the late afternoon, a group of us would have a quiet drink with Les Biffle, the Secretary of the Senate, who was very informative and very reliable. But he wasn't a Press Relations man; he was just an official who was candid. Today I think there are more Press Relations men in the Congress than reporters covering Capitol Hill, and there are probably more Public Relations men in Washington than newspapermen. The problem is that the politician has developed such a worshipful attitude toward these techniques that he feels there is no longer a necessity to practice what should be his basic art, the craft of politics, which, in turn, is the profession of leadership. That's what a politican is for! Instead he regards his job as the practice of public relations. I think that it is rather significant that the rise of the public relations men has coincided with the decline of the politicians.

QUESTION:    You may be right in saying that people are not listening and that the typical person is very skeptical of what he hears but suppose somebody spoke the truth; I am afraid most people wouldn't even listen to the truth.

REEDY: It is very difficult to sort out these days, but I think most Americans would finally judge that whatever was said that accorded with reality would be the truth. Of course, people are skeptical and they have a right to be skeptical. If words have been "pretested" and public addresses have all been "assembled" by public relations men, by speech writers, by motivational researchers, and by psychologists, it is not surprising that the audience pays little attention. I do not want to listen to that kind of speech anymore than I want to live in B. F. Skinner's box and I doubt whether I am unusual. The age has seemed to pass altogether when politicians wrote their own speeches. I myself don't think they should even write them. I think they should get up and give them off-the-cuff because when a man is asking for my vote I want to know what he really thinks, and what he really feels. I am perfectly willing to forgive him any minor slips that he may make. But the fact is that when you see a political

leader on television today, the whole
thing is merely a performance. The
speech has been prepared and at least
ten people have had a direct hand in it;
lighting and make-up experts have been
consulted; and each word has probably
been submitted to Batten, Barton, Dur-
stine, and Osborn and three other firms.
All of this automatically lowers credibility and I believe this is one of the major
factors in the decline of the democratic
dialogue. Frequently, a political debate
resembles two computers talking to each
other. The situation reminds me of a
story I heard a few weeks ago about an
automated atomic facility that had been
built in England. The engineers installed
a computer which was designed to dial a
telephone number and report any break-
downs because human beings had been
completely eliminated from the plant.
The day finally came when a part broke
down and the computer dialed the telephone, the phone rang, and the answer
came: "This is a recorded announcement
—the number you have called has been
changed to 347–8692." It was seven or
eight weeks until officials discovered the
breakdown. I am afraid that is what

most of our political communication is like.

QUESTION: If the typical Senator and Representative has a PR man, as you say, and a Press man on his staff, who would you recommend to him? Would you recommend that he fire these two people and reduce his operating costs or should he have another kind of specialist?

REEDY: I think he ought to fire them and get a couple of political experts in his office. You know the last man I knew that really did it was the late Senator Everett Dirksen, who for all of his faults had one quality that really endeared him to me. He never wrote a speech; he never once corrected the record; he refused to edit his remarks at the end of the working day. On one occasion, when an obvious typographical error crept in (somehow "now" became "not" or the other way around) he agreed reluctantly to have it corrected for what is known as the Permanent Record. I think that political leaders would perform their duties much better if they concentrated on hiring staff members who were politically acute and politically sensitive. Their task, after all, is political leadership and this means leading human beings—not columns of figures.

*QUESTION:* What do you think the news media could do about this gap?

*REEDY:* Newsmen do the best they can and the written press does rather well. It's a more difficult question for television, which does not have the time space. One of the real problems with television is that it has not worked out techniques for conveying ideas. It is not capable of carrying any more than very brief bulletins; it does not have the capacity to really probe into, behind, and under the various words that are being said. But the written press is tending more and more to a type of treatment which rounds up past events and puts them in some sort of perspective. This makes it increasingly difficult for manipulative techniques to prevail. The latter depend upon convincing the audience that it should be oblivious to the past and concentrate only on what is being said right now.

QUESTION:     From your past experience, you were in-
              volved in lots of press conferences, and I
              suppose there are some tricks in them
              that the average person doesn't know.
              Are questions planted?

REEDY:        They are planted from time to time and I
              always thought this was a silly practice
              and I wouldn't do it myself, except on
              very rare occasions, because there is sel-
              dom a real point to it. Anybody with a
              reasonable amount of knowledge of the
              press can sit down the night before and
              write out twenty questions and be abso-
              lutely certain that eighteen of them will
              be asked and perhaps all twenty. The
              basic point of the press conference, how-
              ever, is that as long as it's on television
              the President dominates it so thoroughly
              that it really would be rather foolish for
              him or his assistants to plant things. He
              is standing physically on a higher level;
              he is flanked by the American and Presi-
              dential flags; the setting inspires awe;
              and every single newspaperman when he
              arises to ask a question knows that he is
              being viewed by 110–120 million peo-
              ple. He will be rather genteel about his
              questions. He doesn't want to look like a

lout rubbing the President's nose in some triviality. The President can very easily skip from person to person and there cannot be any follow-up questions. The modern press conference format is a very bad one. It's one in which the President has such complete control inherent in the situation itself that there is no need for any tricks. They are not necessary.

QUESTION:    What would you recommend as a substitute for that? There is merit, it seems to me, in having the President have to respond to real people.

REEDY:    In the first place I would extend the format to an hour. And then I think the President should have two kinds of press conferences. Once a month, he should have a one-hour appearance on television. An hour is enough time to allow for follow-up questions. But then, I think, at least once a week unexpectedly he should call in whatever reporters are out in the lobby and just open himself up to questioning without television. I believe the public would get more of the President's thinking out of that than it

does out of television. The very presence
of television cameras is an inhibiting factor. There are anywhere from 250–450
reporters in the audience. Each one is
anxious to get in his own question. A lot
of them show up primed with questions
from their publishers. When a journalist
has a question from his publisher, he has
just got to ask it. This means that there
is no sequence, there is no continuity,
and at the end of the conference the reporters all run out of the room with
about twenty first paragraphs and nothing to put under them. I believe a mix-
ture would produce something of great
value.

QUESTION: We have a problem, as readers of newspapers, that a reporter will take out of context an answer that a Senator or President has given and make a quotation
that makes a headline but isn't.

REEDY: Well, what is meant by "out of context"?
This is an old, old problem. Politicians
are always complaining that newspapermen take them "out of context" and frequently they do. But usually, when I in-
vestigate such complaints, I find that the

political leader is really concerned because the newsman put his speech *into* context and frustrated a public relations ploy. There will always be some foul-ball news stories and they should not be excused. But I am much more interested in the faults of politicians than the faults of newspapermen. If a newspaperman makes a mistake, my future and my children's future are not bound to it. If the politician makes a mistake, it can mean catastrophe.

QUESTION:    Has there been a decline in the press over the past few decades?

REEDY:    Do you mean a decline in numbers or in quality? There has been no decline in numbers. There are just about the same number of daily newspapers today that there were forty years ago. There has, however, been a decline in the number of competitive newspapers, and this is a very serious trend. Cities that once had four or five or six newspapers now have two or three at the most. And the reason that there has been no decline in numbers is that the gap has been taken up by the rise of suburban papers such as those you have out here on Long Island. The real problem, I think, is the lack of competitive papers, which means that, generally speaking, the average community in terms of the printed press gets its news from one source. That I regard as very bad. That is a problem.

QUESTION: Could I make a remark—I am a lot older than you are, but when you say Roosevelt, I have to think of a first name.

REEDY: Sorry, in my generation there was only one Roosevelt.

QUESTION: If I may correct you in one regard, it was Eleanor's uncle and not her father, I mean not her husband, that used the expression "malefactors of great wealth."

REEDY: You are right. I meant that Franklin had a few like it.

# CHAPTER 3

## WHO WILL
## BELL THE CAT?

*Dr. Knudsen:* Welcome to the third, and I am sorry to say the last, of this year's Pegram Lectures. I think we are all rather eager to hear who is going to tell the Emperor that he has no clothes on and I give the podium right away to Mr. Reedy.

WHAT WE are going to explore is the question of who will tell the Emperor he is wearing no clothes or, to put it another way, who is going to bell the cat.

In a very real sense, I believe the cat is going to be belled. Dr. Knudsen, in some of our conversations during the past week, has commented a number of times that I am considerably more optimistic than I was at the time I completed my book on the Presidency. That is true. But it is true in a very special sense. The conditions that I described are still very definitely in existence. I was talking to a Congressional assistant today who commented on my book and said that he sees all of the same tendencies in the present administration, but in an accentuated form. I believe that is correct. There is all of the same shrinkage from reality and all of the isolation of the Presidency. These forces are still at work. But I think that at this particular point in our history, we are rediscovering the resiliency of our institutions; the capacity of human beings to respond and to devise counter-forces to those in our society which seem to be headed toward disaster or at the very least toward a deterioration of most of the values which we, in western civilization, hold so dear.

In the course of these lectures, I have reviewed for you the tendencies within the Presidential office itself to become more and more separated from human beings. The fact is that the office, to begin with, is essentially a monarchical office—monarchical because the founding fathers really knew no other form of government. What they were trying to do was to establish a king who could not be a tyrant and they succeeded very well. They did not, because they could not, reckon with the modern age of mass society with its staggering problem of trying to hold together a nation of somewhat more than 210 million people—a nation that has become increasingly dependent upon a degree of technology so high that it takes years and years to master merely one of the multiplex skills that are essential to keep a society going. There is a tendency in such a society to seek controls through impersonal means. Leaders try to reduce human beings to integers, to objects that can be counted, to units that are amenable to types of discipline which an individual will not accept. It is natural for such leaders to regard the means of mass communication as essentially mechanisms for social manipulation.

When I look at the scene about me today, I find that all of those tendencies, all of those trends, have been accentuated and are even stronger now than they were three years ago when I finished my book on Presidential leadership. Part of this, I think, stems from the election of a President who, as a person, has a highly introspective personality. Even back in the days before he rose to the position of power, Mr. Nixon was a man who lived to a great extent in psychological armor. When a man who is naturally isolated by temperament is placed in an institution which removes him several degrees from humanity, the obvious outcome will be a man who is even more isolated than his predecessor. I believe that the layers of insulation around the President have been increased. The White House staff today, I would estimate, is about three times the size of the staff that was in residence at the time I was a member of it. This statement is based upon a head count made by a friend of mine about a year and a half ago. He checked out for me the Press Office, and it was three times the size of the Press Office over which I presided. He checked out the National Security Council

Office, and it was about three times the size of the National Security Council Office over which Walt Rostow presided. It is a good rule of thumb that within the White House, if one section or one branch increases its personnel, all of the others will increase by approximately the same degree. There are factors of prestige involved, and a section chief cannot maintain his or her position without holding command over an appropriate number of people.

Nevertheless, I do not find the picture altogether somber. The isolation of the Presidency is increasing, but we are also witnessing within our nation the rise of countervailing institutions. I do not believe that this is the result of conscious design on the part of men and women who have accepted my analysis. Instead, I think it is due to the operation of certain natural laws in society that we do not fully understand. When human beings are confronted with a set of circumstances that place them in an intolerable position, they have a tendency to react, possibly for the wrong reasons, but nevertheless toward the right goals.

I long ago gave up any concept of attempting to rewrite our Constitution or to reform the basic structure of our government. I do not think that this is a profitable method to pursue. When we discuss society, we are discussing human beings to whom any change whatsoever is a terribly disturbing factor. Even desirable changes, even alterations that are obviously good, create insecurity and too many new problems. Frequently, they collapse simply because they disregard the deeply felt human need for continuity of social forms and social customs.

The French are a case in point. After the Franco-Prussian War, they rewrote their Constitution and established a form of government which I personally think, from the standpoint of an objective analysis, was one of the best in history. They copied the British model primarily, but not having a royal family, not having a king, not having anybody with the mystique that is essential to a chief of state, they established a parliamentary form of government in which a premier would be responsible for the day-to-day operations of the affairs of the French people with an elected president to carry out the duties of a Constitutional monarch. Inside of eight months they were in trouble. They were in trouble because they had not reckoned with the fact that no governmental system is going to work unless it is accompanied by political institutions and political forms which are in accord with the political realities of a society. Such institutions and forms cannot be legislated. They must arise out of the natural workings of political forces. This is one element which, in my judgment, has been overlooked in most academic studies of government. In the political process, there are forms of human communication; there are laws of what people will do and why they will do it; there are forms of acquiescence that cannot be measured and cannot be categorized and which come into being solely by an evolutionary process. They cannot be altered at will.

The basic problem in France, of course, was that they

did not have the institution of party discipline. There is no way one can "enact" party discipline. They did not have the concept of accommodation. And again, there is no way that one can enact a concept of accommodation. There is no formula under which one can order human beings to be sensible and to make essential compromises without which no government can endure. These are qualities that arise out of the experience of a people, of centuries of working together and of smoothing the rough edges, of learning the terribly difficult art that all human beings must learn—how we can live together in the same country when many of us do not like each other very much.

The British solved the problem because they had eight-hundred years in which to make their government work. They started in a period when the problems of the island were rather simple; when they did not have to worry about invasion; when smog and pollution were not even gleams in somebody's right eye; when problems of taxation were relatively simple; when the problems of the public welfare were almost nonexistent. And step by step by step they proceeded to build political institutions that were in accord with their form of government. I think they did extremely well. But as soon as another nation tried it—another nation that had gone through a totally different history and which had a different intellectual heritage—the whole system broke down. I think we must realize that here in the United States we must live with what we have as far as our basic charter of government is concerned. At this late date, we cannot make violent changes in our Constitution without creating many more problems than we would solve. This does not mean that we need be helpless in the face of the forces that are tending to break down our society or that we cannot find ways and means of correcting what has gone wrong. But we must make the changes within the framework that already exists. I believe there is sufficient flexibility for this to be feasible.

To me the most interesting factor of the last two years has been the revolt of Congress. This revolt, as is true of most revolts, has not been particularly rational. I think, by and large, the basic cause is that the members of that august branch of our government are just tired of having somebody step on their toes. I doubt very seriously if there are deep philosophical motives behind what they are doing. But in a sense that is irrelevant. We must deal with society as it is and with all the human beings that make it up—people with aggressions, with quirks, and with desires for their own place in the sun. The healthiest thing that has happened to us in the last ten, fifteen, or twenty years is that Congress has finally decided that it has been deprived of its place in the sun. And indeed it has.

Huge budgets, so great and swollen that very few Congressmen can really follow them and cut appropriations intelligently without destroying the country, have seriously weakened the fiscal authority which was such a tremendous part of the checks and balances that the founding fathers built into our system. For example, in a budget of 200 billion dollars, there really are only about 30 or 40 billions over which Congress can exercise control. The balance must be voted almost automatically. Congress cannot refuse to appropriate the money that is necessary to pay the interest on the public debt. Congress cannot refuse to appropriate the money that is necessary to pay veterans' pensions. Congress cannot refuse to appropriate the money that is necessary to pay for our farm programs. I could give you a long list of such items which involve solemn obligations and contracts of the United States government. Congress simply cannot step in and abrogate those contracts. Furthermore, there is not very much that Congress can really do about the defense budget.

Every member of Congress knows that if he votes against the President on any foreign policy issue and things go wrong, then he will be blamed by the public. Usually, in foreign policy matters, things go wrong. The world is like that. On the other hand, if he votes with the President and things go wrong, then the President is the man whom the country blames. The legislator can always say, "Well I had my doubts but I voted to back my President." His constituency is quite likely to accept such an alibi. The result is that from a practical, political standpoint it is a difficult thing for any member of the Senate or the House to oppose a military or a foreign policy appropriation request. About the only place he can do it is in the field of foreign aid, because here there is something the average American believes he understands.

The power of disapproving the President's appointments has never been very effective. A Senator will usually conclude that if the President wants to appoint a man who is unworthy, this is the President's headache, and not his. As a general matter, the members of the Senate will vote to approve almost any Presidential appointment, unless the man has been caught with his fingers in the till clear up to the elbows.

The power of impeachment is an ultimate power. We have only tried it once in our history, and there we discovered that it is too great a power to have much practical use. No one is going to use a sledgehammer to swat a fly or a mosquito. As a general rule when Presidents become crosswise with the rest of the country, it is not because of burning issues such as venality, corruption, or treason, which is the sort of thing the impeachment power was intended to cover. It is usually because they have gotten out of step politically with the rest of the nation. No one is going to impeach a President for that.

I think for a long period of time members of Congress have felt themselves to be in a position where they could really do very little to bring Presidents into line other than to thwart them in their domestic programs. To thwart a President on his domestic programs in the last thirty or forty years was really not to bother him very much. This is because we are living in an era when Presidents regard their place in history as something that will be determined by what they do in the foreign policy field, and, generally speaking, proposals for domestic legislation have had a hollow ring to them. There has been a tendency to present Congress with a laundry list of recommendations, most of which were dictated by overly simplistic views on what is needed for re-election. This attitude has contributed to disillusionment on the part of the American citizens, a disillusionment which, according to a research team at the University of Michigan, has meant that as many as two-thirds of the American people no longer trust their government.

For a number of years, the situation seemed hopeless. The division of powers envisaged by the founding fathers appeared hopelessly overbalanced in favor of the Presidency. However, it has developed recently that there are, within our Constitution, certain soft spots, areas that are only now beginning to be probed, and they are extremely interesting areas. I am referring to a series of bills that have been introduced in the last few months, some of which I believe have a genuine chance of passage. There is, for example, Senator Fulbright's bill which would strip White House assistants of what now amounts to a virtual immunity from being questioned by Congress. Such a law would not do the job completely of course, and it should not do it completely. The President could prevent the appearance of any one of his assistants before a Congressional committee merely by certifying in writing that this was a question of executive privilege. I am all for that. I believe that the President should have the right to confidential assistants who are truly confidential. But when the National Security Council staff has reached the level of 140 people, I simply cannot regard such people as "confidential assistants" to the President. When the Press Office staff has reached the level of 32 people (to be fair I am including stenographers and receptionists), I simply do not believe that all 32 are confidential assistants to the President. They should be subjected to the same rules that govern other federal government employees. As they now operate, they are shielded from adversary legislative questioning, and I believe the mere assertion of Congressional rights to secure information from them would force the President to pay some attention to the other branch of the government.

There are a series of bills that have been introduced by men of such widely varying political outlooks as Senator Javits of New York, Senator Eagleton of Missouri, and Senator Stennis of Mississippi—men ranging about as far over the political spectrum as possible. All of these bills are intended for one purpose, and that is to bring back under the control of the Congress the authority to send our soldiers out to fight. This is one of the areas in which Presidents over the last forty years have accumulated an enormous amount of power because a new world situation has arisen which is not covered by the Constitution. All of us know the classic formula. Only the Congress has the power to declare war, and I have heard many lengthy debates as to why we did not declare war in Viet Nam and why we did not declare war in

Korea. What is not commonly understood is that war is more than a matter of fighting. War is an issue of a legal status. A nation that declares war does so because it is making a total national commitment to victory. It has determined that it is going to crush the enemy and completely frustrate his will to resist. In the modern age I am very, very doubtful that we will ever again have another war in the classic, legal sense. We are now sending men out to shoot at other men and using our armed forces to exert force upon another power as an instrument of foreign policy rather than a genuine commitment to war. Under these circumstances it is entirely possible to commit a tremendous number of troops to combat, such as we did in Viet Nam and Korea, without a formal declaration of war. There is every reason to believe that this pattern will remain as a guide to future policy even after Viet Nam and Korea have been forgotten.

Congress is beginning to react to this situation. The bills I have named are an effort to write legislation which will bring this new form of conflict under control. The authors recognize the fact that no force can prevent a President from committing troops to combat as long as he is the Commander-in-Chief of the Armed Forces. But a law can provide periodic Congressional review after the fact with Congress reserving the power to recall the troops if, at a certain point, they determine that further hostilities should not be conducted.

This is an extremely significant matter. If this were merely the reaction of one or two Senators, or one or two House members of somewhat advanced views, I would not take it very seriously. But when I find men as widely diverse as Senator Javits of New York and Senator Stennis of Mississippi both thinking along the same lines and introducing bills that are roughly similar, it is clear to me that there is a major force at work and that something more is at stake than an individual point of view. That men of such different backgrounds and with such different roots should converge indicates to me that the institution which was supposed to check the Presidency is stirring. I think the probabilities are that some such legislation will be passed and will become a part of our basic law. Even if it does not, however, the mere fact that it was considered will have an impact upon the White House. The President cannot fail to be impressed by such an expression of sentiment.

There are other interesting new developments. The various legislative moves that have attempted to curtail the fighting in Viet Nam, or to order the President to remove troops by a certain date, have been defeated. Americans who regard the conflict as a major tragedy have interpreted these votes as resounding defeats to those who want to get out. They simply do not know Congress. I have been fairly close to the House and the Senate since 1938, which, in human terms, is a long period of time. To me, the fact that such motions can muster 35 or 40 or 45 votes is little short of a revolution. It is unprecedented for so many Senators to oppose a President on basic foreign policy.

Even in the case of foreign aid, which is so complicated that there is no simple way of analyzing Congressional votes, there is a growing revolt against the President. It is in this revolt that I think we may come to our salvation. I do not mean that Congress will take over and run the country, because it cannot. The founding fathers did not intend the Congress to manage anything. Management is not the role of Congress. There is no possible way that the House and Senate could handle the day-to-day running of our government. But the point is that in these actions, some of which are illogical and many of which should probably be defeated, the President is beginning to see the rise of a peer group. He is finding that there are men he must take into account. Here we must consider a basic question of the psychology of the political personality.

The political personality really listens only to those people whom it must take into account. In the practical, day-to-day cross fire of politics, the arguments, the pleas, the kind of debate that might win a prize in a high school forensic society are of rather secondary importance. What counts is whether the discussion is among a group of men who *must* pay attention to each other because each has power. If the President must pay attention to the Congress, then there will be a breakthrough of the wall of isolation with which he has been surrounded. Legislative assertiveness is growing. It is becoming more and more a factor in our life. Ultimately it can lead to certain changes which will not alter the structure of the written Constitution but which will govern the actual working of the Constitution.

The British have not operated from a written document. They have proceeded on a practical basis. The most important step was the successful parliamentary effort to pry the Cabinet and the Prime Minister loose from the King. I would not want to pry loose all of the instruments through which the President exercises his power. It would be both wrong and impractical. But I do think that it would be very healthy, and would give us a breath of fresh air, if some of those instruments were subjected to greater checking and supervision, and this is going to happen.

In the years that lie ahead, it is possible that more and more Cabinet officers will spend more and more time answering very sharp, very hard, and very hostile questions from members on the Hill. It is also possible that the executive branch will surrender more and more information.

Again, the information is not the basic issue of importance. I believe that if Congress gets all of the information that it is asking for, it will be very unhappy indeed. If I wanted to frustrate a member of a Congressional committee that was trying to get some information out of me as an executive officer that I did not want to give him, I would load a 2½ ton truck with every scrap of paper that I could find and send it to him. I have already come to the conclusion that historians are going to be frustrated by too much paper piled up in too many

Presidential libraries. This may also be the way that Congressional Committee chairmen will be frustrated. Nevertheless, the mere fact that Congress is asserting the power to obtain information can compel the President to come to terms with the legislative branch. Should that happen, we will be moving back toward the type of democratic government and free-flowing communication which I believe is the key to a healthy federal structure. Once that is achieved, then we have the key to something else—to communicating with each other in a mass society.

Practically speaking, I think we all know that it is not possible for the President of the United States to communicate directly with 210 million people. All of the techniques of mass communication—television style, pretested words, "scientific" polling, motivational research—have arisen because he simply cannot shake hands and exchange views with more than a few at a time. Fundamentally our task is to try to reshape our government so that the pyramid of society, which now ends up with the President in a lonely eminence, becomes a series of pyramids in which we, as individual citizens, have leaders with whom we can communicate and who in turn can communicate on up to the top. We cannot, even the group in this room which includes some very prestigious people, assemble around a President and insist that he listen to us. But it is quite possible for us to influence representatives who in turn may influence other representatives who ultimately will be able to insist that the President come to a room and listen to them.

This is a development that I believe is now under way. And in the course of it, the Presidency is going to become a very different thing than it has been in the past. The job will remain. The title will remain. We will probably go on electing the man the same way we have in the past. But I also believe the loneliness, the armor, which has distorted our whole political and social and economic life can be removed and will be removed. Once again we will stand forth as a nation that has a genuine political life and no longer is merely getting by from day to day, wondering how we will sustain the ordinary housekeeping of our government.

So, Dr. Knudsen asked, who is it that is going to tell the President that he has no clothes? Many people have been telling the President over the last few years he has no clothes without too much effect, but the voices are growing stronger and I believe they are beginning to penetrate. Possibly some one of these days, they will penetrate to the point where the leader of our nation becomes what he was intended to be, a man who really leads, a man who talks with us rather than at us, and who is capable of leading a democratic society.

Thank you, and let us see if we have any questions.

*QUESTION:* I was wondering if you had read *The New York Times Magazine* section of October 17, in which there was an article about Rene Dubos, a past speaker here. I thought it might amuse you to hear a paragraph of that. I quote, and this is Mr. Dubos speaking: "That fellow with all the hair who is President Johnson's Press Secretary, George Reedy, said to me, 'How do you go about converting this into steps that government and the people should take—one, two, three, four, six' " (this was about pollution), and I think you have done a very good job of giving us the one, two, three, four, five, six about the future of our country. And I thank you very much.

REEDY:     I remember that evening very well. It was at the Woodrow Wilson International Center for Scholars and I am very fond of Mr. Dubos who, I think, has performed a tremendous job in clarifying our picture of the universe. But I was concerned about a series of steps that he was proposing, and I simply couldn't see how these steps related to action by the people. I still don't see it, frankly. But it was an enjoyable evening. Thank you very much for your comment.

REEDY:     Does anyone else have any questions? Over here?

*QUESTION:*   I would like to know if you think the demonstrations that people make in Washington or the letters that housewives write make an impact.

*REEDY:*   Yes, very definitely! The question is do the demonstrations, the students in Washington, and the letters written by housewives and other people make an impact. The answer is yes, very definitely. But again you have to realize that everything can wear out its welcome and that letters must be genuine letters. As a former Congressional assistant, I have spent considerable time handling mail. It is amazing how soon one develops an eye that detects the difference between a letter written by a person who really means it and a letter that is the result of a writing campaign. I can recall the days of the Bricker Amendment when we were receiving about 5000 letters a day. There were eleven from a clinic in west Texas—the wording was identical, the typing was identical (because they had all been typed by the same stenographer), the spacing was identical, and nothing varied but the signatures. Eventually I found out that an organization

in Chicago was circulating form letters
which doctors were signing and sending
to Congress. I think that this is one of
the reasons doctors have lost most of
their influence with Congress. When I
first arrived in Washington, they were the
major lobby in the city and could get almost anything they wanted. I think their
mass support of the Bricker Amendment
broke their political back because Congress came to the conclusion that they
were political sheep who couldn't be satisfied. I think the medical profession has
a real problem on its hands trying to re-
establish some political prestige which it
now does not have. The Bricker-type letter does not have any influence. As for
the demonstrations, I am familiar with
them. I have a son who is a part of the
New Left, and each one of these demonstrations usually winds up with anywhere
from 45 to 75 kids staying at our house;
helicopters buzzing over my roof every
morning to check out the "revolution";
and long-haired youths sleeping in bath-
tubs, on the steps, and on the couches. I
believe they had a tremendous influence
at first. I think they will have less of an
influence in the future because most of
our youth seem to have decided that

these particular tactics are not effective beyond the point already reached. Nevertheless, the big demonstrations really had an impact, something like throwing a brick through a plateglass window. Sometimes there is a certain value to that tactic. Mr. Nixon, very ostentatiously, ignored the first one. You may recall that he watched a football game on television. Then, on the second demonstration, he met some of the young people by the Lincoln Memorial and demonstrated his knowledge of modern youth by assuming that they were interested in surfing and football when they were in Washington in connection with Viet Nam. Nevertheless he changed his tactics. I believe he really is trying to get out of the war now, not fast enough for my taste but I am not going to fault him altogether for that as we were pretty deep in Viet Nam already and I can understand why he may think it is necessary to disengage slowly. The trouble, however, is that the demonstration is too massive a method for what we need in our society. We need a much quicker response from our leaders. I don't mean to have our leaders changing their policies every time a Gallup poll changes, which really able political leaders won't do anyway. We need channels of communication to the top that salvage the one thing of value of the old political machine. If I sound nostalgic about the old political machine, don't be deceived. I cannot stress too heavily that it was corrupt, that is was an ugly thing to look at, that it was based upon a way of life that I don't think very many of us would value very highly. But I said there was one thing of value to it—it was responsive. And I think we have to re-establish that responsiveness so that we do not have to have 200,000 or 300,000 young people go to Washington to demonstrate popular desires which I believe should have been apparent to our leaders without demonstration.

QUESTION:    I want to know if you feel, as I do, what we have lost at the local level in communication between the people and the next level of elected power, which is the town government.

REEDY:    I haven't addressed myself to that specific problem in these lectures. I have written some articles on it. I do think that this is one of the places where we went off the track. I also think, however, that that is where we are getting back on to it the fastest. One of the developments that fascinates me is that during my early days in Washington, my friends were interested only in the Presidency and in the very highest levels of the Cabinet and the Congress. They really did not care about their neighborhood or about where they lived or about such local issues as sewage and school bonds. Shortly after the war, I began to detect a change. I would visit friends and I would find the wife running a mimeograph machine because she was interested in a school board election; the husband running for the school board; and the older children cranking out literature on the meaning of a bond issue. I think that to some extent we have established or re-established some sense of a local tie. You can also see it in our newspapers. It's a rather startling statistic that we have as many newspapers in the United States today as we had forty years ago. This surprises many people because a large number of newspapers have shut down. What has happened, however, is that the big newspapers in the center city have closed but have been replaced by a new type of newspaper flourishing out in the suburbs. I think it's regrettable that the center city newspapers have shut down because this means lack of competition and I can detect an almost immediate dedication to mediocrity when a newspaper loses its competition. I think it's one of the worst things that can happen. But the growth of suburban newspapers is one of the healthier trends in society. It does not, however, answer the thing that concerns me the most, and that is the tremendous gap between the local level and the people up on the top which is what I have addressed myself to in these lectures.

QUESTION: You made a remark that in the last thirty years most of the Presidents or all of them thought their place in history would be determined in the matter of how they handled foreign affairs. I still have the distinct impression that President Johnson actually felt frustrated by foreign affairs, he felt his place in history was actually going to be determined by the "Great Society" and the bulk of internal affairs.

REEDY: I am not going to discuss President Johnson too much because I don't think it's fair. But I think I can say that there is no question in my mind whatsoever that the "Great Society" was what really interested him. Lyndon Johnson was a man who thought that all of the world's problems could be solved by giving people greater access to electric power, by placing an adequate floor under wages, by placing an adequate floor under farm prices, by assuring everyone an equal right to a job, and by giving everyone an education. I think education was his principle fascination. The man was almost superstitious about education. I believe he thought it would cure chilblains. He found that he was frustrated because of the Vietnamese War and I think he sensed that his place in history was probably going to be determined by it. I am afraid he read the signs quite rightly and while I don't pretend to know what history is going to say in the future, I think it's a pretty good bet that he'll rise or fall on Viet Nam.

*QUESTION:*    I would like to hear a little more about the budget. My sort of feeling outside of the large buried part of the iceberg that you can't touch is that you have a whole series of committees in Congress, each one of which has interest in a little piece of the budget. But really there is nobody that looks at it as a whole or shapes it as a whole; everybody has his own little constituency and on that basis how are they going to do anything other than go along with the President and the President's budget management.

*REEDY:*    This is one of the problems of course. Congress has been trying for years to find some way of actually bringing the budget under control. The Legislative Reorganization Act of 1947 has a provision in it which has never been observed once; that at the beginning of the year Congress is to lay down a legislative budget which includes an estimate of the amount of revenues that will be received by the federal government and an estimate of the amount of spending. It is a physical impossibility. I am not even certain the Budget Bureau could do it. The House of Representatives does a rather good job on individual parts of the budget. When I say a good job, I do not mean that the decisions are necessarily correct but they know what's in it and act accordingly.

QUESTION:    Can you comment on the proposal for revenue sharing?

REEDY:    I am a bit worried about revenue sharing because it amounts to giving the federal government more control. After all these years in government I have become convinced that control follows money. I do not know where the states and localities are going to get the money they need. I am afraid that the temptation will be to go in for revenue sharing, which of course we are already into in a very, very deep way.

QUESTION:    Throughout our history our system has been quite erratic in throwing the best men to the top. Do you see any trends in this direction?

REEDY:    I think the most perceptive comment on that question came from Gary Wills in Nixon's Agonistes who says that our system does not necessarily produce the best men, but that it always produces appropriate men, which means that if the nation is confused, we get confused men. Now the presidential primary system is characterized by a number of problems. People vote differently in the primary than they do in the general election. For example, in any kind of a primary, George Wallace can always roll up a tremendous vote, sometimes as high as 40–50 percent. In a general election, in the same area, he'll only get about 10 percent or 11 percent or 12 percent. Furthermore, the primary election does not allow a second choice to emerge and in the political world so much depends upon the second choice. At any gathering of people you will always find that there are four or five points of view. It is rare to have a genuine majority. Usually most of the participants in a political struggle discover they cannot have their first choice. Then it becomes a question of their second choices and which of these various choices factors out as the man who will be nominated. Sometimes this process throws up people like Warren G. Harding and sometimes people like

Adlai Stevenson, who I do not think would have been nominated in 1952 if there had been a straight-out national primary. I once believed that great crises produced great men. I have since seen too many great crises that haven't produced great men.

*QUESTION:*  Is it not necessary to be wealthy to run for anything these days?

*REEDY:*  No! What you have to do, however, and I think it is unhealthy, is to have a great deal of money at your command. At the Presidential level, this is not particularly bad. There are very few strings on campaign money at that level. It is the local level that concerns me. I think at the local level campaign contributions usually create a due bill on which the donor intends to collect. But I have discovered that at the top level people give money for prestige purposes. A good example is the series of President's clubs, where the member puts in a thousand dollars in return for a card signed by the President and a steak dinner in his presence. I was fascinated by the discovery that these donors do not think they are buying anything for their money other than the reputation of being a friend of the President. I should add that is all they usually get.

*QUESTION:* If this power structure changes by having the President have his peers in Congress, do you visualize our political structure changing? For example, would there be more party discipline? Also, what happens to the one-party district?

*REEDY:* The one-party districts are pretty well gone. This may seem like an extreme statement to you as I know that here you are living in a very strong Republican area. But you have elected Democratic representatives and there was a period when that would have been entirely impossible. In the South, which was the stronghold of the Democratic Party, there are very few areas today where Democrats are not being challenged by Republicans. New Hampshire or Vermont, once Republican strongholds, now have extremely strong Democratic parties and Maine has not only a Democratic Senator but a man who may be the Democratic Presidential nominee.

The one-party structure is dissolving very rapidly although there are strong holdovers. I believe we may find that a complete dissolution of the one-party areas could be a setback to our political system. There are years of sweeping victories, such as we had in 1936—an election year which almost killed the Republican Party—and I think we were hurt as a result. The basic problem, however, is that political forces have changed and political structures have not changed with them. Today when I talk to people, I find they have a genuine interest in ideology. Political discussions center around the Vietnamese war, ecology, forms of taxation, relatively abstract issues about education. This is a departure from classic American politics. During most of our history political discussion centered on simplistic slogans such as "the demon rum" or "free silver" at 15 to 1 or 16 to 1 (I can never remember Bryan's exact ratio), or "the full dinner pail." Our genuine political structure was based largely upon an intensely pragmatic approach to the governmental process and ideologies were discussed only as entertainment. There are now people in this country who are intensely interested in ideology. There are a number of new elements in the voting equation—the black revolution is, for example, as big a revolution in some respects as Andrew Jackson's. The rise of youth is a genuine force in politics. For the first time, there is a genuine "women's vote," in the sense that women are voting what they consider female interests. When women's suffrage was granted originally, men were frightened by it, but it turned out the women voted just about the same way as the men. Today we are beginning to get the rise of a genuine feminist movement. All of these factors have led to profound changes in our political structure. We have not accommodated ourselves to them as yet.

QUESTION:  You mentioned that people are more idealistic. It strikes me that most people still really think of their stomachs.

Yes, but their stomachs have become more educated. Almost everyone thinks with his stomach. That factor has made a deep impact on history. Why are my people in this country? We had stomach trouble! We couldn't get anything to eat in Ireland. Basically human beings have certain needs. They must have a certain amount of warmth; they must have a certain amount of food; they must have a certain amount of shelter; and they must have a certain amount of respect from their fellow human beings. Any time any set of institutions, let alone a political structure, deprives them of those things, then they will either find a political method, which is essentially democracy, of resolving it, or will resort to revolution. Now, once we reach the stage where people are assured of food, warmth, shelter, and a reasonable degree of prestige, then more complex issues arise. But it is amazing how quickly they evaporate whenever the basic needs are at stake. People are always going to think of their stomachs. There is nothing wrong with that.

QUESTION: Would you please comment on John Gardner's "Common Cause" and what good, if any, it might do.

REEDY: Well, I have confidence that it will do some good because I think John Gardner is a very good man. However, my own reservation about it is that I think it is a little too scattershot. I am always a little skeptical about what is essentially a lobbying effort that seeks only to "do good" and is united on a very broad base. My experience in Washington has been that every lobby that has gone down the drain did so because its objectives were too broad. "Common Cause" strikes me as taking in too much territory.

QUESTION:     A moment ago you used the expression "the rising level of education." Would you elaborate on that thought?

REEDY:     Up to about twenty or thirty years ago, education was by and large something for the elite in our society. You could be reasonably certain that almost anyone in college would be a fairly quiet person. He or she might go out and swallow some goldfish or see how many of their colleagues could crowd into a telephone booth, or indulge in the famous "panty raids" that some of us remember from a few decades ago. But this was merely youthful sap rising in the Spring. Basically, college-educated people were either elite or on their way to becoming elite. In either case they were quite complacent, quite happy with the world around them, and very unlikely to make any serious trouble. Today, a college education has become somewhat of a commonplace. A bachelor's degree is no longer a meal ticket to much of anything except a job as a checker in a supermarket. A BA degree is about the equivalent of a high school diploma when I got mine. Many young people think that they have a right to a college education in the sense that a previous generation thought it had a right to a high school education, and a previous generation thought that it had a right to a grammar school education. At that stage in the development a number of things happen. One of them is that the young people who find that their college education is not as highly valued as it formerly was, do not value it very much themselves. This leads to the surprisingly large number who are just turning their backs on it. Furthermore, mass education opens up possibilities of mass revolt. It gives people a greater degree of sophistication in government and government policy.

This sophistication does not necessarily lead to more valid political ideas, but it does complicate politics. It adds to the political process an articulate group which is not under the same economic pressures as their elders and therefore more difficult to organize.

# CHAPTER 4

## CONCLUSION

IT IS NEARLY a year since I completed the Pegram lectures at Brookhaven Laboratory and the passing days have, to my eyes at least, shed considerable light on the convulsions in our society. I do not pretend to see any solutions. But the shape of the forces with which we are confronted is taking on more comprehensible form.

This has not been a truly stormy year. If anything, it has been almost serene in contrast to the riots and demonstrations which were shaking our campuses and our ghettoes such a short time ago. However, it has been a year of surprise in which one political party nominated its least likely candidate and the other political party, long based on dogmatic anti-Communism, found its leader opening broad highways to Communist China and the Soviet Union.

Perhaps the greatest surprise, however, has been the emergence on the national scene of women as an independent, political force—not just women voting but women voting as women and insisting on their share of the rewards and favors that normally accompany political power.

The full scope of this force is still unclear. Leaders of a new movement always tend to extreme statements in order to be heard by the power structure, and the power structure in its turn always tends to interpret the statements in an even more extreme fashion. The result is that "Women's Liberation" is treated in many quarters as a joke—something to do with "bra burning," trying to make "the old man diaper the kids," and praying to God so "She will help you."

There is a rich vein of the comic underlying all human activity and the women's lib movement is no exception. But the politicians who are surviving are those who have made the discovery that it is no joke. They are treating it as a force that is here to stay and struggling manfully (my apologies to Gloria Steinem) to master such ungainly expressions as "Chairperson," "Ms." and "role reversal." The two major political parties are shoving their women forward almost rudely and there are more female candidates on the ballot than I can recall in any other campaign.

The impact is not limited to political activity. Some of my friends in industry are now searching frantically for a "house woman" on their executive payrolls, just as a few years earlier they were searching for house Blacks. I doubt whether any real change has been made as yet in the sexual composition of business leaders as a group, but it is very clear that a real change is in the offing. Every business meeting that I have addressed in the past few months has included at least one woman vice-president of something-or-other whereas a few years ago all such audiences were totally male.

I do not intend to plunge too deeply into an analysis of the women's lib movement. Probably, because of age and sex, I lack the qualifications to understand it in an ultimate sense. But however different they may be physically, men and women share the quality of humanity and some community of understanding is possible. Within that community my own thought processes have been enlightened by a number of incidents that lead me to believe that the new status of women, aside from the merits of the case, has been brought about by the same fundamental forces that are disturbing our society so deeply.

Let me give two examples which are not isolated but are typical of many recent experiences.

A few months ago, I addressed a group of businessmen who had been brought to Washington for a series of briefings on the workings of the government. In the course of the discussion, one of them asked me whether I took seriously "all these women who want to be like men." Off the top of my head, I replied:

"I do not believe that there are many women who

want to be men but I believe the country is full of women who are sick and tired of doing a Vice President's work for a secretary's salary."

I was startled by a sudden burst of applause from the one woman present (a regional manager in the west for a national corporation) who bounced up and down in her chair with excitement she could not contain. It was spontaneous and, in a social hour that followed, I found out why. She had lost her husband a number of years earlier and been left with two children to raise. She had succeeded in doing so and both were now through college. But the price had been job after job for which she had received pay $2,000 to $3,000 less than would have been accorded to a man in the same position. She had no patience with arguments that a woman "head of a household" is de-sexed. "If they want me to be 'womanly,' then somebody has got to pay for raising my kids," she said.

A few weeks ago, at a social gathering with a few very conservative, Catholic families, I casually mentioned my surprise over the depth of feeling of so many women over the abortion issue. My point was simply that I had always felt intellectually that a woman had the right to make such decisions herself, but as very few women had ever said anything about it, I had discovered only recently that their feelings ran strong and deep. This provoked a heated defense of the anti-abortion laws by one of the men who argued that abortion was simply murder which no one had a right to commit.

"That is not the point," said a woman present. "I cannot imagine wanting an abortion myself but I think that if I did, it should be between me and my doctor."

"Suppose your husband wanted the child?" asked the man.

"That's different," she replied. "He is responsible for helping me raise the child. But no other man has the right to tell me what to do. He is not sharing the risks with me."

I am not offering these two examples as statistical proof of anything. I do not know how many women share the feelings of the two ladies (although my social sense of smell tells me this is widespread) and I have no intention of making a numerical survey. The interesting point is that these women were confronting a condition which did not exist in the past except for the very poor and the very oppressed—and they belonged in neither category. They were facing the reality that in the modern world a woman of a "respectable," middle-class background can be left alone with heavy obligations and absolutely no help in meeting them.

This is a reality which runs counter to the mores of our society. Most of us have been raised on a mystique which is based on the concept that the family will step in and take over the woman's burdens. At one time this was a valid concept, and it still is in significant areas of our life. But for the "middle class," which so many pundits regard as the driving force of a nation's politics, the validity is decreasing rapidly. In this world, women are either on their own or likely to be on their own without warning.

The simple, observable fact is that the family is no longer a partnership unit. It can be held together by love, decency, habit, or mere horror of loneliness. But should any of those ties deteriorate, the bonds can be severed easily. There is no longer the unbreakable cement of a compact in which people undertook to work together in order to live. The family has been separated from the process of production for survival.

I am not a sociologist and I have no intention of making an in-depth analysis of the family structure. My only objective is to consider the impact of readily apparent social forces upon our political dialogue. I am no authority on why it happened or how it happened. But the disintegration of the family as an economic unit has broken down old constituencies and created new constituencies, and constituencies are the lifeblood of the political process. They cannot be ignored.

In the past, it has been a rule of thumb among the more skilled politicians that women will vote just about the same way that their husbands vote. In retrospect, I realize that the rule could have been reversed and been equally valid. It was not a question of the woman following the lead of the man. The reality was that of a whole family—grandfather, grandmother, father, mother, son, daughter—looking at the world from the same platform and therefore coming to similar conclusions. That platform might be a farm or a tailor shop; a smithy or a grocery store; or possibly just a company house in a grimy mill town. It did not matter because the members of the family were sharing each other's problems. There was an identity of interest and therefore an identity of outlook.

Among blue-collar workers, the platform may still exist. But, contrary to the predictions of Karl Marx, they are a diminishing breed. The more common picture is that of people who live totally different lives from eight in the morning until seven in the evening and whose daily contacts may represent something of an ordeal. I saw this phenomenon in its worst manifestation a few years ago, and the memory remains a nightmare.

A friend in New York City invited me to spend the night with him on Long Island. We boarded the train at an early stop where very few passengers were picked up, and he led me to the bar car "because there is something I want you to see."

I found out what it was at the next stop. The doors to the car came dangerously close to buckling from the pressure of the packed mass of male humanity as the wheels ground to a halt. In they came streaming, like cattle through a chute; sweating, cursing men ripping off their jackets and battering their way with their elbows for a favored position at the long counter. Orders came thick and fast—orders for two drinks at a time which could be slugged down from each clenched fist in time for another order before someone in the rear had succeeded in displacing the customer in the favored position. There was little or no conversation—just the me-

chanical motion to the hip pocket to pull out a wallet
and pay; the replacement of the wallet; the two quick
gulps and then the second order.

At each stop, a small group would stumble out of the
doors to the station platform where wives were waiting
to drive them home. I did not go to the end of the line,
but I assume at that point the conductor strained the
contents of the car through fine cheese cloth and delivered what was left to the women. (A suburbanite later
told me that many of the wives had spent the afternoon
getting crocked also but I have no way of confirming
this. If so, I cannot blame them.)

This is obviously an extreme situation and I doubt
whether it describes any overwhelming group of citizens
—not even the commuters on the Long Island Railroad,
most of whom do not travel via the bar car. I cite it as
the ultimate in the "lives of quiet desperation" led by so
many families today where the husband vanishes in the
morning to do something incomprehensible 40 or 50
miles away and returns in the evening ready for nothing
but an alcoholic snooze. This is not a moral preachment
to be followed by an exhortation to "do better." It is
merely pointing out the evident fact that life in suburbia,
the residential area for most of the second-level leaders
of our society, is not conducive to an identity of outlook
among members of the family.

Meanwhile, what is happening to our young people?
Alcoholic fathers and indifferent mothers are nothing
new in history. What is new is the status of children as an

economic liability. This we have not seen before on a large scale. In the past, and that includes the very recent past, children were assets who took their place as producing members of the family as soon as they had sufficient strength. They were welcomed not just because they were loved but because they could lighten the burdens of the father and the mother. It was not always a pretty picture and there were parents who exploited their children as mercilessly as any mill owner of the Industrial Revolution. Nevertheless, regardless of aesthetics, it was a system that promoted cohesion and unity.

Today, we have children solely for our own emotional satisfaction—because of our need to love. This is a relationship which we idealize, and for those parents who do have the capacity to love, it is a relationship of great beauty. But there are many parents who do not have that capacity, and when they make the discovery, they have no position to fall back upon. There is nothing left but burdens and debt.

The more significant point, however, is the impact upon the child even when the love is real and enduring. Sooner or later, he or she discovers the liability status, as children are extraordinarily acute when it comes to human relationships. It cannot be a very happy moment in anyone's life when one learns that one is being maintained on the same basis as a pet dog or a goldfish—to satisfy the master's emotional needs. I do not have the skill to plumb psychological depths, but I have the strong feeling that student unrest, the "hippie" movement, and the "drop out" phenomenon have a direct relationship to this aspect of our society. It has been my observation that those of my friends who have been grieved by what they regard as their children's ingratitude were those who loved their children the most and needed them the least.

For the purposes of these lectures, it is not essential to trace the alienation of the young people back to its roots. We need note only that what is happening to them is a manifestation of the separation of the family from the production process. Our objective is to go on from there to determine whether this separation relates to our problems and to the decline of the democratic dialogue in our society.

If we push this thought further, it is impossible to avoid the discovery of an even more disturbing development. It is not just the family but men and women themselves who are being separated from the production process. There are increasing numbers of human beings who are totally nonessential, except as consumers, to the economic system that feeds them, clothes them, and shelters them. Many are still unaware of their status since industry, which needs consumers much more than it needs production workers, has found executive "jobs" for them shuffling papers in the same spirit that WPA workers raked leaves during the depression.

I am not presenting this phenomenon as any great discovery on my part. It is a well-known condition of modern civilization, and the shelves of the behavioral sciences are thick with studies of proposals to expand recreation, adult education, and intellectuality as a substitute for meaningful work. Perhaps some of those proposals are viable. I hope so although most of them seem rather "artsy-craftsy" to me. Nevertheless, the facts are apparent. We have created surplus human beings (usually described as people with more leisure time), and it is bound to have an impact upon our political structure.

Karl Marx wrote that the determining factor in political activity was the relationship of men to the production process. As in so many other things, this is an instance in which he seems to have been partially correct. What he did not consider, however, was a situation in which men would be totally irrelevant to the production process. The revolutionaries of his time were intellectually capable of overthrowing with ease such concepts as private property and inherited nobility because technology had reached a stage where they could envision a world without such institutions. Technology had NOT reached a stage where they could picture a system without the "work ethic," so they contented themselves with devising schemes under which *everyone* would work. In a world in which intellectuals are busy constructing ideal models of a society in which *no one* works, it is hardly surprising that Marxism seems so quaint.

The full implications of such a society are difficult to discern. To most of the leaders of the rapidly rising constituencies, what is happening is a broadening of freedom. Abbie Hoffman, the Peter Pan of Bolshevism, is ecstatic in describing the new era in which people will do their own thing. Gloria Steinem thinks of a world in which women will have the full opportunity to achieve their full potential as human beings. Germaine Greer speaks of the time when children will be "liberated." And many of the "women's lib" leaders are already planning to liberate men from the tyranny of "the male hang-up."

I have not the slightest doubt that all of these movements represent strong currents of social change which cannot be stemmed, even though I have reservations as to whether the leaders are describing them correctly. The more interesting thoughts to me, however, lie in an examination of the word "liberation." It is being used in a somewhat different sense than when it was applied to Blacks, where it meant freeing them first from slavery and then from discrimination so they could join society on a basis of equality. What is intended here is "freeing" people from social institutions which in the past were approved by people at all levels of society.

To put it more specifically, what we are talking about is the "liberation" of people from a series of allegiances —from marriage, from the family, from the church. It is a movement of rapidly increasing success because we are in the process of creating a society which does not tolerate allegiances to anything but itself. It is a society which refuses to recognize as sanctified any relationship other than the impersonal interdependence of people who are held together only by the mysteries of cost accounting.

Almost unconsciously, we are slipping into the world foreseen by Aldous Huxley in which "everybody belongs to everybody else" which means that nobody belongs to anybody and therefore everybody belongs to the state.

The difference, of course, is that Huxley conceived of such a world as full blown—one in which there could not possibly be any dissent. We are living in a world in which there are forces moving in the direction of his forecast; forces which are resisting the trend; and forces which are totally indifferent to it. It is a universe of "gaps," of which the credibility gap is only one. Far more important are the "gaps" which make it impossible for people, generations, and constituencies to even talk to each other.

Recently, I had a painful conversation with a young intellectual who has "advanced views" on anything and everything. His current concern is to strike the shackles of superstition and "male chauvinism" which have enchained women for so many centuries. As a contribution to the liberation cause, he and his wife tried the experiment of "role reversal," which was not a very satisfying enterprise because she could not devise any method of impregnating him and he could not devise any method of producing anything but a meal. All they really discovered is that every type of work is drudgery when it has no purpose.

The major impact of the experiment was upon his parents, pious, old-world Jews who grew up in an era when people *knew* who and what they were. The very real agonies of this young man are totally incomprehensible to his father and mother, who can only interpret this type of behavior as morbidity and who now say the traditional prayers for the dead for their son.

The young man's dilemma is unsolvable. He believes he should have a "meaningful" relationship with his parents, but he cannot participate in what he regards as "superstitions" from which he has been "emancipated." Their world is one which he cannot consider as "relevant." Actually, he has not been emancipated from anything as he was never a part of the society in which his mother and father lived. At best, he was a "star boarder" in their house—the recipient of love, affection, warmth, shelter, and food and the provider of nothing which was necessary to the family's survival except the hope that some day a proud man and a proud woman could say: "Our son, the doctor!"

It would be a simple matter to dismiss this situation as an instance of pure neuroticism. I have not heard of very many people who are playing "role reversal" and I doubt whether the women's liberation movement can count on many supporters of such passionate intensity. Nevertheless, neurotic behavior, even among a few people, is frequently a good barometer for measuring strains in our society and revealing forces that might otherwise go unnoticed.

The question of "relevance" is increasingly upon the minds of intellectuals in the modern world, and it has nothing to do with neuroticism. It flows from the fact that they are being declared "surplus" at an increasingly rapid rate and having forced upon them the discovery that they really have nothing to do. These are bleak days for English, history, philosophy, and political science Ph.Ds. One professor teaching political science at a small college recently showed me a list of universities to which he had applied, hoping to improve his status. What he had discovered was that for every job opening there were at least 15 applicants "and in one case there were 65."

"What good was it for me to get my Ph.D?" he asked, bitterly.

The only logical answer was "no good whatsoever." He had not really been educated in the sense of being helped to cope with life. He had been trained—trained to turn out other Ph.Ds, who in turn would train other Ph.Ds to turn out Ph.Ds, and so on, ad infinitum. It is a system which bears a suspicious resemblance to the "chain letter" swindle that swept the country during the depression years.

The chain had reached its inevitable end. The professor in question was unusually skilled at his job, which was evident from the fact that he had one in a buyer's market. But he had been brought face to face with the fact that he really was not doing anything essential to the survival of the human race. He was merely a replaceable part in an economic machine which had manufactured so many replaceable parts that his continued functioning was merely accidental.

Were this particular professor a genius, of course, he could find some method of controlling his own destiny. But although he is highly intelligent, he is not a genius. Therefore, he is turning his efforts toward preserving what he has and has become a leading spirit in organizing professors for "collective bargaining" with university administrations. This is taking him another step along the way—into the field of organizational politics where he is wading deeper and deeper into caucuses, manifestoes, and political conventions. Into this arena, he is bringing all the bitterness and frustration of a surplus man plus the effectiveness that flows from experience in being articulate and at ease with parliamentary procedure.

He played a major role in securing a pro-McGovern delegation from an Eastern state but now finds himself strangely ill at ease with the election process. He is afraid that men running for office tend to "compromise" their principles and make "too many deals." The next step in his development will probably be the "no politician can be trusted" syndrome, which can be the predicate for some very explosive ideas.

This man cannot be ignored. In an age of mass production intellectuality, he can be duplicated thousands of times; and each one of his counterparts has been trained in the instruments of leadership. They represent a new class of rootless intellectuals, and while the class will probably never become large, it is certain to be influential. It is intelligent, articulate, aggressive, and frustrated.

It is looking for allegiances and not finding any of them very satisfactory. We tend to think of professors and academicians as gentle and ineffectual. At best, the picture never had more than limited validity. What will happen, however, if there is nothing for them to do but live on the charity of society?

It is not beyond the scope of human ingenuity to devise means of sustaining surplus human beings economically. Nor is it impossible to plan activity which will occupy their time. The intellectuals can be "put to work" making studies of human alienation; the business leaders can be sent to conferences on marketing and sales; the young people can be required to take a compulsory BA and perhaps some graduate studies. The nagging problems will still remain. How do we sustain humanity when human beings have been separated from the production process?

For the present, of course, all humanity has not been separated from the production process. It is still possible to walk down the streets of any large city and observe that most people really have something to do that contributes directly to human survival. Although it seems to be on a diminishing basis, we still require cooks, carpenters, truck drivers, electricians, production workers, engineers, doctors, lawyers, and even intellectuals who are in that category because they have an irresistible compulsion to ponder ideas.

These are the people who are not yet caught up in the centrifugal forces of alienation which we have been describing, although I sense an uneasy feeling among them that their days may be numbered. They are not at all ready to accept the propositions which are so deeply embedded in the consciousness of our youth, our professional intellectuals, our advocates of unisex. Their perception of the universe is quite different. They see a world that is disintegrating because people lack moral fiber and do not have the courage to "stand up for what is right." As far as they are concerned, the intellectuals have had their chance and have failed.

The result of all this is what I see as a new class division in our society—one that is as deep and as bitter as any we have known before. It lies between those who are surplus to the production process but who still have prestige and those who are essential to the production process but who generally lack prestige. This is a stratification which has led to considerable bitterness and a brand of politics which can take on a high degree of ugliness.

This polarization seems to me to have colored all of our politics for the last few years and is the dominant theme in the 1972 election. It is not simple to describe because human affairs are never orderly, and the phrase "dominant theme" does not mean the only theme. Neither does it mean that the polarization will be decisive in shaping the outcome. We are dealing with complexities which are not amenable to simplistic solutions.

Nevertheless, we are confronted with a new class in society and it cannot be ignored. It was responsible, I believe, for the nomination of Senator McGovern as the

Democratic Presidential candidate and for the retirement of many of the leading members of Congress. It is doubtful whether it can win the election * but I am convinced it is here to stay as a major factor in American society for many years to come. As time goes by, it will pick up more experience and increase in political potency. By 1976, it should be formidable unless its ranks become too divided by factional strife.

To the conventional American politician, this new class is baffling. He (I use the word advisedly to make it clear that I am describing the conventional politician) is accustomed to groups that present clear-cut demands susceptible to political action. He has confronted Blacks who wanted civil rights legislation; farmers who wanted parity payments; unions who wanted higher minimum wages; businessmen who wanted accelerated depletion. In each instance, he was able to perform a type of social cost accounting which weighed the relative strength of the protagonists against the price of acceding to their programs and came out with a roughly satisfactory answer, or at least one that kept him in office.

The new class of surplus human beings does not fit into the classic formula. Its only common denominator is that it has been dispossessed from the traditional production process, and it is held together more by style than by aspirations. There are no 10-point programs, no legislative strategy, no specifics for social action that can serve

* This was written prior to the elections in November, 1972.

as a basis for bargaining. In fact, the new class is not interested in bargaining. It wants to change society itself,
not just the rules by which society operates. Fundamentally, this is a group seeking to recover its soul—a goal
that cannot be achieved by legislative enactment or executive decree.

For the moment, the full impact of the new class is
felt only in the Democratic Party. But this is because
that party is out of power and has not succeeded during
the last four years in producing a dominant leader. The
Republicans, in my judgment, will face many of the
same forces in 1976 when their only dominant leader becomes ineligible for re-election and the GOP is up for
grabs. I doubt whether the impact will be quite as great
because, traditionally, Republicans are not as yeasty. But
it will be there and I do not envy them the experience.

The most significant reaction to the new class up to
this point has been the Wallace phenomenon. It has been
a mistake, I believe, to attribute the Alabaman's unexpected popularity solely to racism. This was probably the
force which gave him his start in local politics. But his
base is much broader today. Primarily, it consists of
those who still have a stake in life—who still possess allegiances to the institutions that are shrinking under the
assault of new-style economics. They are trying to keep
what they have and it is impossible for them to understand those who do not have it.

It is highly unlikely that Mr. Wallace would have gone
on to the Presidency even if he had not been shot in

Maryland. He lacked the respectability that Americans still consider a prerequisite for high office. Whatever help racism may have been when he was running for Governor of Alabama, it is a handicap now—not because our country has been swept by the spirit of universal brotherhood but simply because racism, however much it may still be practiced, is no longer "respectable."

During his campaign, however, Mr. Wallace sounded themes that had a deep appeal: "I am going to take those pointy-headed intellectuals and throw their brief cases into the Potomac River"; "The Editor of the New York Times thought that Fidel Castro was an agrarian radical when every cab driver in Birmingham knew that he was a communist." It was a reassurance to people who work with "hard facts" that theirs is the world of reality and that the "new forces" in society are merely corrupting phantasms that can and should be exorcised. Many of my friends dismiss Mr. Wallace as a mere demagogue playing upon the fears and prejudices of the uneducated. I believe they have missed the point. What he is doing is rallying those who have a stake in a social order that may be passing but is still potent.

It is equally a misapprehension, in my judgment, to interpret what is happening as a continuation of the struggle between the left and the right wings of our parties. In the context of the 1970s, such words are as obsolete as "easy money" and "hard money." "Wings," whether left or right, operate within a common framework in which accommodations are possible—in fact, inevitable. And one of the most marked developments of 1972 is the size of the groups that can no longer "live" within the traditional party structure. Mr. McGovern has been trying to breed his followers to more conventional Democrats, but so far his success has been minimal.*

In the past, there was a type of politican who specialized in holding the political parties together. The late Speaker Sam Rayburn was a specialist in this field for the Democrats as was the late Senator Everett M. Dirksen for the Republicans. They were technicians who could calculate to a millimeter the precise point at which a compromise could be struck which would maintain political solidarity even though it might leave everyone vaguely dissatisfied. It was a form of power brokerage ideally adapted to a system in which political parties are primarily coalitions rather than ideological groupings.

Many people have nominated themselves as successors since these leaders passed away, but somehow they have not been replaced. Senator McGovern obviously hoped that Lawrence O'Brien could perform the function of pacifier for him, but the early returns are not encouraging. I would suggest that this does not reflect any lack of skill on the part of Mr. O'Brien, whom I know to be a very able man. It is closer to the mark to assume that he simply does not have the necessary material at hand with which to forge unity. He is dealing with people who do *not* want to be united—even if the price is the loss of an important election.

* This was written prior to the elections of November, 1972.

Mr. Rayburn, in his political prime, was dealing with political groups who disliked each other intensely but who still had specific programs over which they could bargain. Southerners were bitterly antipathetic to pro-labor legislation but still needed Northern help to sustain cotton and tobacco price supports. Westerners disliked Eastern-inspired credit policies but still needed allies to rescue reclamation projects. There were literally dozens of issues out of which an astute man—and the late Speaker was very astute—could forge alliances, with the help of such able pupils as Lyndon B. Johnson, that would at least take his political party through an election. It was a heavy strain in view of the civil rights controversy which dominated his era, but it was possible even though there were chips that would not always stay in place.

No amount of political skill can keep people together who are uninterested in trading. The new class of surplus people is in this category. It is not just unwilling to trade. It is seeking goals that are not amenable to the trading process. One cannot swap 90 percent of parity for an end to the Vietnamese war; 10 reclamation projects for an improved ecology; 20 Hill-Burton hospitals for improving the status of women. And would it be possible to call off a lettuce boycott in return for a higher degree of participatory democracy?

The merits of the goals sought by the new class are not in question in these lectures. What we are exploring is the impact that the quest for such goals is making on our society. It becomes evident at the outset that for the time being the demands are indigestible—not because they are necessarily wrong or difficult to attain but because they are of a new order. This is not an instance of a group asserting its right to a larger share of the social pie but insisting that the pie be reassembled and rebaked in a different pan.

It is something of a commentary on the human species that the pressure groups most troublesome to a society are those that are driven by something other than economic self-interest. Men and women who are seeking a larger share of the material goods and services that the system has available can always be persuaded to settle for something short of their goals on the plea that they must come to an accommodation with others who are seeking the same thing. If peace and serenity were the only criteria, the ideal society would probably be one in which all powers were centered in the hands of cost accountants.

Lest anyone misunderstand, I hasten to add that I would not regard such a society as ideal. There are aspects of the human personality which cannot—and should not—be satisfied just because physical appetites have been quieted to a reasonable degree. It is not possible to quantify such qualities as justice, hope, and excellence and allocate them on the basis of a profit and loss statement. They are nevertheless real and will continue to move people toward political action.

Our economic system today is dominated by the techniques of cost accounting. The process of quantification is taking over more and more of our lives and reducing most individuals to the status of a social security number. Normal human intuition is subordinated to a reverential respect for mathematics. Elections are forecast upon the basis of polls, and government programs are guided by cost/benefit ratios rather than by administrators. The computer has replaced the Delphic oracle as the prime font of wisdom and, judging by what it told our leaders in the early days of the Vietnamese War, it is a poor substitute.

The interesting factor is that in its triumph the age of cost accounting has produced its own antagonist. It is the combination of the computer plus technology that has resulted in the new class of people that have been separated from the production process. They are the elements of the new constituency that cannot be bargained into the temporary accommodations that keep a society going. It is not clear just what the outcome will be. But it is clear that the future will be troublesome.

The question is the extent to which our system retains sufficient flexibility to withstand the shock. In the past, we have demonstrated many times over our capacity to adapt to changing times and changing circumstances. We have survived the frontier revolution in the age of Jackson, the Civil War in the age of Lincoln, the economic revolution in the age of Roosevelt. Our record is good.

This time, however, there is reason to question the adaptability of our institutions. The age of mass society has encouraged a greater isolation of our leaders from the people and the substitution of mass techniques of control for the older and more individualistic style of personal politics. The current occupant of the White House is not even attempting to deal with the new constituencies in our society. Instead, he is deliberately addressing himself to the reaction—a strategy which could well be successful this year whatever may be the outcome down the road.

Somewhere along the line, in the swift pace of change in society, we seem to have lost our ability to communicate with each other. The polarization described above —between those who have been eliminated from the production process and those who are still a part of it or think they are—has meant a great gap in our perceptions. It is not so much that we disagree but that we do not even know what we are disagreeing about. We are not speaking the same language.

As an educator, however recent, I have discovered already how deep one of those gaps can be. There is no experience quite as revealing as talking to the parents of an incoming freshman class and then talking to the new students the next day.

The parents are out of the post-World War II era when college education, for the first time in our history, became reasonably available to large groups of people other than the elite or the very determined. Their degrees were passports to economic advancement—certificates which enabled them to live better than *their* parents without challenging the fundamental assumptions of the past. They are doing their duty by enabling their sons and daughters to receive their certificates, but they are troubled with nagging doubts that the process will work out the same way. Their apprehensions are justified.

Within a few short months, their children will return to them unrecognizable in both appearance and outlook. The neatly pressed trousers and the "off-to-school" frocks will have been replaced by faded blue jeans and T-shirts; the male hair will be down to the shoulders and the female hair down to the waist; the Oxfords and the heels will have been replaced by sneakers. Far more important, however, the parents will find that they are not regarded as "doing any favors" for their young.

Those of the students who have turned left (the number is far smaller than parents fear) will regard college as merely another institution with which the "establishment" seeks to enforce conformity. The majority will regard it as merely another baby-sitting structure in which they have been parked because their parents do not know what to do with them.

In either case, the parents and the students will inhabit separate universes, as incapable of understanding each other as residents of Flatland and residents of the three-dimensional world. The problem is far more than the identity crisis which has afflicted every human being at some stage of life throughout history. Nor can it be traced to "what they are being taught at *that* school," as so many of the parents suspect. The unhappy reality is that most of the children *have* been raised as emotional luxuries surplus to the survival needs of their fathers and mothers. It is a status which they resent, and they express the resentment at the first opportunity.

This is not what I regard as the only major gap in our society. There are many others of equal—and possibly greater—importance. I cite it here only because it is the one to which I am closest at the present time. But it bears a close affinity to all the others in that it also rests upon the depersonalization of human relationships which has attended the separation of human beings from the production process.

In the days of my youth, those of us who were members of the "left" shared a dream of a society in which men and women would be relieved of toil. It loomed before us as a beautiful world in which there would be no "artificial" allegiances; no barriers to the fullest expression of the human personality; no chains of superstition that had been forged in the past. There would be ample food, ample medical care, ample shelter, ample education for everyone, and the affairs of mankind would be ordered in a rational manner by objective experts whose only interest would be the enhancement of the general good.

It still seems like a good dream to me. I am no more fond of drudgery than I have ever been and I recoil with the same horror from the hangovers of discrimination and superstition. I have spent considerable time in countries where food, medical care, shelter, and education are not even minimal, let alone adequate, and I have nothing but scorn for those who believe the inhabitants will suffer from "cultural shock" if their living standards are raised by a modernized economy.

Nevertheless, now that part of the "brave new world" is upon us, it seems to me that there was one factor which we did not take into our calculations. Human beings must have a purpose in life in order to be serene, and "leisure time" activity is not enough to fill the need.

For the time being, we can only say we are confused. It is obvious that the allegiances which held our society together in the past are crumbling rapidly. It is not possible to foresee what will rise in their place. In the past, human beings have always succeeded in building new institutions to replace those that have fallen. I have faith in this historical process. But in our present society we have yet to succeed in doing so and still await the day in which we will have certainties upon which to rely. Until that day, we must all find the spiritual resources within ourselves to make life worth living.